# THE
# SAMARITANS OF MOLOKAI

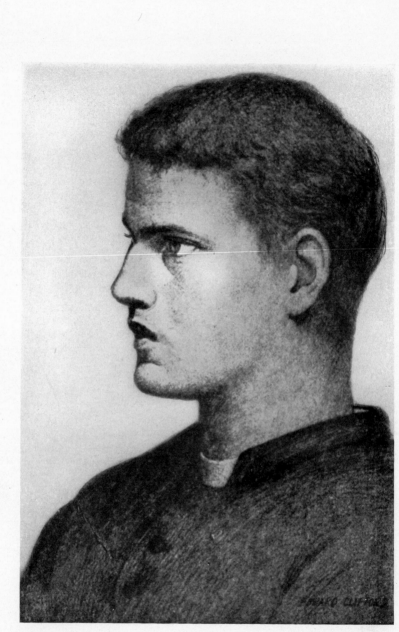

FATHER DAMIEN
*(from the portrait made by Edward Clifford)*

# THE
# SAMARITANS OF MOLOKAI

### THE LIVES OF FATHER DAMIEN AND
### BROTHER DUTTON AMONG THE LEPERS

*By*

## CHARLES J. DUTTON

*Illustrated*

## DODD, MEAD AND COMPANY
NEW YORK                    1932

PRINTED IN THE U. S. A. BY
Quinn & Boden Company, Inc.
BOOK MANUFACTURERS
RAHWAY.     NEW JERSEY

TO

THE MEMORY OF

FRANK C. WATERBURY

WHO WAS BROTHER JOSEPH'S FRIEND AND MINE

# INTRODUCTION

MANY a book when completed is quite different from its author's first conception. When the letters and documents relating to Ira Dutton (Brother Joseph) first came into my possession, I meant to write only the life-story of the now famous lay brother. But it soon became evident that to do this without describing Father Damien's life at Molokai as well would be like trying to roof a house before laying its foundations. Brother Joseph was not only the friend and associate of the "Apostle to the Lepers," but also the administrator of Damien's estate and his successor in the work of the leper colony. His recollections of the last three years of Damien's life are unknown to the general public.

It appeared, moreover, that if the book was to be complete it must include a third element—the historical background of leprosy, particularly the history of its ravages in medieval England and the desperate attempts of Church and State to deal with it. Thus was the work broadened in scope.

Two-thirds of it is based directly on the hundreds of letters and documents that Brother Joseph saved during his forty-four years at the leper colony, together with the copies he made of his own letters. During his last illness he knew that this book was to be written—

indeed was already in process of preparation; he discussed it with the priest who nursed him, and much of the material came directly from him before his final breakdown. As a preliminary to the actual writing, more than one hundred and fifty pounds of letters, documents, and clippings were read and arranged in their proper order. In Brother Joseph's own letters were great gaps, sometimes of years, representing various periods in his life that he wished to keep hidden, events that were barely hinted at in his writings. It is these periods that have, in the past, occasioned so many wild guesses and fantastic stories, and around which many unreliable news articles have been written. Fortunately we have been able to fill these gaps from sources independent of Brother Joseph himself, sources that are unexceptionably authentic. Brother Joseph never kept a diary.

The writer of biography may treat his subject in any of three ways. He may adopt the plan that is so fashionable today, of interpretation in the terms of modern psychology; Brother Joseph offers a great temptation to use this method. Or the writer may fit his subject into the times in which he lived, using the era as background for the person. Or—lastly—he may seek only to tell, very simply, the life-story of his subject, presenting the man's character and career honestly and with little comment of his own. It is this last method that has been adopted here. The author believes that the important thing about Father Damien and Brother Joseph is not the psychological motives that might have actuated their lives, but the moving story of the charity and devotion that made up those lives.

A large part of the basic material was turned over to the author by the Rev. John Wynne, S.J., of New York, to whom Brother Joseph had sent it several years before his death; it included the papers mentioned in his will. In one form or another some—a very little—of this material had been used in rather obscure publications; but by far the larger part had never been printed. To Father Wynne's interest and kindness we owe the use of this material.

Another large collection of letters was in the possession of the late Frank Waterbury of Des Moines, Iowa. Mr. Waterbury was for many years a close friend of Brother Joseph, and the two carried on an extensive correspondence. It is these letters that provide us with details about the early life of Ira Dutton (Brother Joseph) which are not to be found elsewhere; the contents now see the light for the first time. Several incidents hitherto unknown, also relating to his boyhood days, have come from his relative, Miss Ethel R. Simmons of Edgerton, Wisconsin; her mother, who is still living, knew Ira Dutton as a boy and kept in close touch with him all his life. It is from such material that this book has been written, and we feel safe in saying that at one time or another we have had in our possession virtually every record of any kind that relates to Ira Dutton.

I wish to thank the Iowa Library Commission in

particular, and also the Iowa State Medical Library and the Iowa State Library, for their kind services during the preparation of this book. To other institutions I am also indebted: the Wisconsin State Historical Society; the Library of the Catholic University of America; the Library of Congress; Adjutant General's Office, Madison, Wisconsin; the Surgeon General's Library; the University of Minnesota Library. Many persons deserve thanks for the loan of material and letters. I am particularly under obligation to the following: the Sisters of the Convent of the Good Shepherd in Memphis, Tennessee; Rev. John G. Dutton of Agawam, Massachusetts; Judge Stout of Clarksville, Tennessee; Rev. Joseph Hanz of St. Jude's Parish, Beloit, and head of the Dutton School; Mrs. Emily Moeser Minter, Librarian of the Public Library of Janesville, Wisconsin; Mrs. J. M. Semmes of Memphis; Miss Nina May Rhoades of Honolulu; and Orrin Sutherland of Janesville.

To Helen Harper Aten, reference librarian of the Iowa Library Commission—my secretary—I owe a debt that cannot be expressed in words. Her enthusiasm and eager interest were shown not only in the necessary research work she did, but also in the many readings and final checking of the chapters. Without her help this book could not have been completed, and in a real sense it is as much her book as my own.

CHARLES J. DUTTON.

Des Moines, Iowa,
July 15, 1931.

# CONTENTS

CHAPTER                                                       PAGE

   I  SOWERS OF PESTILENCE . . . . . 1

  II  THE LEPER AND THE CHURCH . . . . 18

 III  FROM OCEAN TO OCEAN . . . . . 39

 IV  DAMIEN THE BUILDER . . . . . . 60

  V  GREATER LOVE THAN THIS . . . . 85

 VI  VENOM . . . . . . . . . 105

 VII  A WISCONSIN BOYHOOD . . . . . 124

VIII  FIGHTING IN THE CUMBERLAND . . . . 142

 IX  THE SECRET YEARS . . . . . . 158

  X  THE PENITENT . . . . . . . 183

 XI  FRIENDS AND CO-WORKERS . . . . . 197

 XII  IN HARNESS . . . . . . . . 218

XIII  "LIFE HAS BEEN GOOD TO ME HERE!" . . 239

XIV  BROTHER TO EVERYBODY . . . . . 259

     BIBLIOGRAPHY . . . . . . 281

# ILLUSTRATIONS

Father Damien . . . . . . *Frontispiece*

FACING PAGE

Towering cliffs near the leper settlement . . . 16

"The Old Man of Molokai" . . . . . 32

The leper settlement at Molokai . . . . . 49

Father Damien's old altar, which is preserved in the
present church . . . . . . . . 64

Father Damien two months before his death . . 88

The office and cottage of the manager . . . 96

Father Damien's grave beside the church at Kalawao 104

Abigail Barnes Dutton, Brother Joseph's mother, at
the age of 77 . . . . . . . . 128

Lieutenant Joseph Dutton . . . . . . 144

Joseph Dutton, 1867 . . . . . . . 144

The present church at Kalawao . . . . . 161

Leper boys at the cottage . . . . . . 161

Looking seaward from the Baldwin home . . . 176

The flag at half-mast on Memorial Day . . . 193

The Baldwin home for lepers, Kalawao, Molokai . 200

A group of boys with their directors at the rear of
the Baldwin home . . . . . . . 200

Brother Joseph and other Brothers . . . . 208

Brother Joseph and leper boys . . . . . 216
xiii

FACING PAGE

Brother Joseph in the garden near his cottage .   . 225

The last picture of Brother Joseph  .    .   .   . 232

The last card sent by Brother Joseph .   .   .   . 240

In his office at the cottage  .   .   .   .   .   . 248

The Dutton school, Beloit, Wisconsin   .   .   . 256

A reflective mood on Thanksgiving Day .   .   . 264

Hoisting the flag .   .   .   .   .   .   .   . 270

# THE
# SAMARITANS OF MOLOKAI

No golden dome shines over Damien's sleep:
A leper's grave upon a leprous strand,
Where hope is dead, and hand must shrink from hand,
Where cataracts wail toward a moaning deep,
And frowning purple cliffs in mercy keep
All wholesome life at distance, hath God planned
For him who led the saints' heroic band,
And died a shepherd of Christ's exiled sheep.
O'er Damien's dust the broad skies bend for dome,
Stars burn for golden letters, and the sea
Shall roll perpetual anthem round his rest:
For Damien made the charnel-house life's home,
Matched love with death; and Damien's name shall be
A glorious benediction, world-possest.

H. D. RAWNSLEY.

# CHAPTER I

"UNCLEAN! Unclean!" That desperate cry of the leper has rung in the ears of men for thousands of years. The pathetic story of his mysterious and hopeless disease constitutes one of the many pages of history as yet unwritten. We know that the fate of civilization has always been delicately balanced; many a nation destined to rise to greatness has from time to time been threatened with extinction, often by war but just as often by famine or pestilence. The European peoples, for example, were beset by leprosy after the Crusades; and England during the years from 1200 to 1350 barely escaped having her population wiped out by it. This page of history, if not entirely blank, shows but a few lines of writing, and those are legible only to scholars.

Perhaps it is not unnatural that the story of leprosy has thus far remained untold. Until comparatively recent times the general attitude toward the disease combined panic fear with superstition, both of these heightened by ignorance of its true nature. Even today most of its major mysteries are unsolved. We know that it is a germ disease, we have isolated the bacillus—and there we are stopped. What causes it? How is it transmitted? What will cure it? These are

I

all controversial questions, as much disputed now as they were a thousand years ago. Why it is common in some parts of the world and unknown in others—this, too, has never been satisfactorily explained; every attempt at explanation runs sharp against the barrier of conflicting testimony. One fact alone has come down the ages unchanged and unchallenged—humanity's universal horror of the disease.

Universal? No, not quite. Here and there in history exceptions have appeared, Good Samaritans moved by the spectacle of loathsome suffering to subjugate that horror to tender pity and to translate their emotion into ministering activity. Among these were Father Damien and Brother Joseph Dutton of the leper colony of Molokai, whose dramatic and moving careers are the subject of this book. Their service is hardly to be appraised at its true value except as it is set against the background of the history of leprosy. Before we review their work we must search the records of past ages in other parts of the world, gain some sense of that age-long accumulation of horror and helpless fatalism which the Samaritans of Molokai so resolutely defied, bequeathing a story of self-sacrifice that reflects imperishable luster on the Church they served and offers to their fellowmen a unique example of heroic humanitarianism.

Leprosy is an ancient disease, perhaps as old as Man himself. Though its beginnings are lost in the mists of antiquity, authorities agree that it originated in the thickly populated valley of the River Nile, in what we now call the Egyptian Sudan. It is known to have existed during the reign of Hausapti of Egypt, at a date near 3000 B.C. The so-called Ebers Papyrus, dealing with the 16th century before Christ, mentions leprosy as then sweeping through the Negro slave population in the Sudan. This fact would seem to support the belief of many authorities that the bacillus thrives best in a warm, damp climate. But we dare not be too dogmatic on this point, for the disease appears in cold, dry countries as well. Yet there is little doubt that its actual origin may be assigned to the Nile valley.

Early Egyptian manuscripts blame the River itself for the plague. They point out that the slaves and the poorer classes ate quantities of raw fish—often decaying fish—and they try to show some causal relationship between this diet and the spread of leprosy. Even today the "raw fish" theory is believed by some; though, as with so many other theories on the subject, the evidence is conflicting. The doubters cite the fact that tribes in India and Africa who never eat fish are badly afflicted. Probably the most that can be said is that there is some connection between a hot, damp country, the diet of its people, and the spread of leprosy among them. And in any case, we know that the plague first observed among Egyptian slaves increased among the rest of the population and ultimately spread practically all over the world.

The first introduction of most of us to the subject is made through our reading of the Bible. It may be—

as asserted by those who accept the story of the captivity of the Children of Israel in Egypt—that this people got the infection during that period.   But an old tradition says that the Egyptians expelled the Jews because the latter, being badly infected, had given leprosy to their captors; for this story, however, there is scant evidence.   What is certain is that the disease was known in the early days of the Jewish race, though we must bear in mind that much that the Bible calls leprosy was really not leprosy at all—it is generally agreed that the word translated "leprosy" (zaraath) applies to other skin diseases as well.   There is indeed much controversy as to the true nature of the disease mentioned in the Old Testament, for all the wealth of detail given about the examination and treatment of the suspected leper.   The familiar Biblical phrase "a leper white as snow" does not fit leprosy as we know it today. Furthermore, though leprosy nowadays is not highly contagious and is curable only in its early stages—and as yet only rarely even then—the Old Testament regulations are plainly based on the premise that it was both highly contagious and readily cured.   The priestly rites enjoined in Leviticus assume that the disease was a punishment inflicted by God, and a few simple sanitary precautions are imposed.   The belief that it was highly contagious is attested by the requirement that the leper's house be torn down and his clothing burned, the leper himself being obliged to take up his abode outside the city walls; and the provision of a purification rite to be followed on his recovery is witness to the expectation that he might be cured.

In India we find leprosy mentioned as first observed about 1400 B.C. The Vedas speak of it as *kustra,* and it appears to have been fairly prevalent, since rules were given for treating it. Apparently it had come from Egypt, brought to India by traders and sailors. Phœnician seamen carried it from Egypt to every country they visited. Hippocrates reports that there had been traces of it in Persia in the 8th century before Christ and called it "the Phœnician disease," saying that it had been spread by sailors. It appears, however, to have been almost unknown to the Greeks in general before 200 B.C., for Aristotle (one hundred and fifty years before that) spoke of it as a very rare disease in his country. We learn from Herodotus that after the Persian invasion of Greece large numbers of Persian soldiers—Herodotus says thousands—remained in Greece, and this would account for the introduction, or the spread, of leprosy there at the later date.

It was unknown in Italy until after the Roman armies had invaded Egypt. But they brought it home with them, and from Italy it was to spread throughout Europe. It was these same Romans that carried leprosy to Germany; after their conquest of Spain we hear of it there; and indeed, wherever the legions marched, they carried the plague with them. In later centuries it was England that was to suffer most, until there came a time when it looked as if eventually every person in the land might be afflicted. This story of the rise of leprosy in England, like that of its sudden and mysterious decline, makes an almost unknown, yet fascinating, page of history.

A common misapprehension on the subject is to the effect that it was the Crusades that introduced leprosy both on the Continent and in England. Voltaire said: "All that was gained from the Crusades was leprosy." And both Astruc and Bach, the earliest authorities, state with conviction that it was first brought into Europe by the returning Crusaders. The error has been accepted and repeated ever since in almost every work on the subject and is still to be found in most reference books. The historians who fall into this error cite the fact that almost all of the larger leper houses in England were opened after the Crusades, and that the laws passed for maintaining these houses, as well as the statutes that fixed the social and legal rights of the leper, were all enacted during the 13th and the 14th centuries. Their facts are correct, their conclusion wrong. For at least a thousand years before the first Crusader returned to his home the plague had existed in England and on the Continent, and five hundred years before the Crusades were dreamed of there were leper hospitals in Europe. Many of the ecclesiastical rules and rites dealing with the leper had been in use long before the 12th century, and the leper mass antedated the First Crusade by many years. That it is safe to say that leprosy was at least common long before the Crusades is suggested by the record of the Welsh king, Hoel Dha, who about the year 945 felt moved to enact special laws dealing with the problem. These not only prescribed a distinctive garb for the leper, but also provided that the wife of a leprous husband was entitled to a separation and that whatever property she had brought to her husband on marriage should be restored to her. The leper himself was treated as if he were dead, all his religious and property rights being taken from him.

What appears to be the truth is that, as the period of the Crusades approached, leprosy, already present in England for the past thousand years, began to assume alarming proportions. How it had originally entered the islands has been suggested. If pre-Roman Britain had little contact with the world beyond the Channel, she was also spared its pestilences. But when the army of Aulus Plautius landed, this isolation was broken. Here was one of the finest armies ever sent forth to conquer—forty thousand seasoned soldiers, veterans of the hard-fought wars in the East. Almost all of them had been to Egypt, the home of leprosy. And as they disseminated the culture of each country they subdued, so also they carried abroad its vices and its diseases. Galen's account of leprosy in Gaul says that it was brought there by Roman troops.

Thus, it is not until after the invasion that we first hear of the plague in the British Isles. It was noted in Ireland in A.D. 432, and by 550 had become epidemic. From 500 onward we find recurring mention of it in the records. The "Chronicon Scotorum," for example, notes briefly that it is increasing in England. How prevalent it was we cannot tell; but reading between the lines we get a picture of a disease that was slowly gathering force. Over on the Continent, Pepin the French king, after long discussion, had forbidden lepers to marry and made leprosy a ground for divorce. By the early part of the 7th century the Church had begun to establish leper hospitals to care for the victims. We hear of such hospitals at Verdun, and later of a lazar house at Metz. In England somewhat earlier—in about 600—a leper hospital was opened in Nottingham, and a few years afterwards another in Norwich.

Though the story of what must have taken place in England from the Roman invasion to about 1100 is far from complete, its gaps can be filled with some degree of conviction. The coming of Roman ways changed the life habits of the Celtic tribes. They had lived in small groups, scattered on hilltops and in deep forests; now they began to herd together in towns. Their former mode of life did not favor the spread of pestilence. Leprosy at worst is only mildly contagious, and while the people lived in isolated groups, communicating with difficulty, a rare disease would make slow headway. But with the beginning of town life and the increasing use of the military roads that the Romans had built, any infection could easily spread, aggravated, of course, by the current ignorance of sanitary precautions. And this is precisely what happened—a gradual increase of leprosy in England up to the time of the Crusades, when suddenly it flamed forth as a huge, menacing plague.

If the Crusaders may not be charged with having introduced leprosy into Europe, it is certain that they were responsible for increasing and intensifying it. For the crusading hosts were made up not alone of ardent and devout souls bent on rescuing the Holy Land from the infidel. These were inevitably accompanied by thousands of men of the baser sort, thrilled by the tales of plunder to be had in the East; and poverty-stricken peasants and villeins, outcasts, prostitutes, camp followers of every kind further augmented the ranks. When this army reached the Near East it reached also the home of leprosy. The disease was common in Levantine towns, and neither in these nor in the ranks of the Crusaders was there any conception of what constituted sanitary living conditions. The result was a disastrous increase of leprosy all over Europe as soon as the Crusaders began to straggle homeward.

The soil on which they sowed this fresh seed was fertile. Just before the First Crusade the western part of Europe entered a period of great economic depression, followed by a failure of crops, and then by famine and pestilence. The population was for the most part undernourished, sickly, and poor; its best stock was drawn away by the lure of crusading ventures; and finally the cost of financing the successive armies sent against the Saracen had impoverished the countries participating. All these represented, of course, the perfect prerequisite conditions for the spread of any plague. It was like a fire that has smouldered for hours and—at the first breath of wind—bursts suddenly into fierce flame.

It is easy to trace the onward sweep of the plague during the 12th century. From Italy it passed to Spain, then into France; it jumped to England, and spread over the greater part of Germany. By the time it had begun to decline in these countries it was increasing in Scotland, Holland, and Denmark. Lepers were to be seen everywhere in Europe. At one time a third of the population were infected. The lepers, being forbidden inside the city walls, congregated at the gates, extending their bowls for alms. Every road and lane rang with the sound of the clappers they carried as a warning of their approach. Daily the leper mass was read in the churches, declaring the living victim civilly and religiously dead. Leper hospitals were myriad. In England, whose people numbered not more than two and a half millions, one-third were lepers. London had 35,000 inhabitants, and one-fourth of them were lepers. All sorts and conditions were afflicted by the hideous disease. There were lepers on the throne and in the armies and in the Church. Leprosy was no respecter of persons.

One potent factor in this frightful situation was the character of living conditions among all classes during the period. From the unpaved roadway, heaped with garbage and offal pitched from the houses, the pestiferous air swept into the home of rich and poor alike. Elbowing the houses were traders' stalls selling half-decayed food of all sorts, and both houses and stalls were perfect breeding-places for any flying germs of disease. What windows there were hardly served the cause of ventilation since they were never opened. Even if they had been, no circulation of air could have been got, owing to the projecting eaves and the narrowness of the streets. Nor was there any drainage. The mud or wooden houses had dirt floors covered with rushes that were not renewed for months on end. Under this mouldy layer of decaying vegetable matter the filth and refuse of the house accumulated, its odor filling the close rooms. England had not yet learned to love fresh air.

As for food, palace fared hardly better than hut. The masses lived chiefly on hard black rye-bread and salted fish or meat. The fish was badly preserved and often half-decayed. There were nearly a hundred fast-days in the year, on which only fish might be eaten, so that this semi-rotten salt fish was a staple diet everywhere. Fresh meat was almost unknown, and when it was to be had could often hardly be called "fresh," and had to be highly salted in order to disguise its putridity. The rye meal used for the bread was commonly hard and old. Vegetables, save for carrots and perhaps cabbage, were not grown. Most persons in that day went their entire lives without eating a vegetable of any sort. Finally—to close this attempt at describing the indescribable—people slept in their daytime clothing, and the poor had for beds only the rotting floor-rushes.

No sower of pestilence could ask for better ground than this.

So violent and widespread an epidemic as leprosy proved to become during the Middle Ages raises a curious problem. What may we fix on as the cause of its spread, in view of what modern science knows of its character? Leprosy has been proved not to be infectious, though there persists a debate as to its contagious nature; even if it is contagious, however, the risk from contact seems to be small. Yet the leprosy that raged over Europe has the appearance of a highly contagious epidemic, carried by human association from person to person and from town to town; and the civil laws and religious ceremonies applying to leprosy were evidently based on the assumption that it was infectious as well. The theory that it is inheritable has also appeared. The author of "Elephantiasis Græcorum," Liveing, doubts whether it was contagious, but goes on to say: "Admitting that the disease is inherited, the effect of this in a few generations would be obvious." But he is wrong; almost all of the modern investigations in the subject tend to prove that it is not inheritable. It is therefore hardly possible to ascribe the spread of leprosy in the Middle Ages either to infection or to inheritance; and even if we admit its contagious character, that risk is too mild to serve as the single and exclusive cause. Probably the real cause or causes of the phenomenon must be considered almost as mysterious as are those that led to the sudden decline of the epidemic after a few hundreds of years.

One of the checks on the spread of leprosy has already been mentioned—segregation in leper hospitals or lazar houses. Before the age of the Crusades there seem to have been a few of these in England and on the Continent. The substantial increase in their number must be credited to those same Crusaders who were responsible for the sudden aggravation of the disease itself. In the Near East their leaders had observed local methods of handling the problem. They had seen many hospitals, some of them hundreds of years old. And on their return to their own countries they encouraged the institution of similar houses in an effort to curb the epidemic.

By the middle of the 13th century there was not a religious order, not a city, town or village in Central Europe, that did not have its lazar house. Every monastery supported one, and they were all crowded to the doors. France alone had two thousand of them in that century, and Louis VIII enacted laws regulating them. Exact figures cannot be obtained for the whole of Europe, but apparently there were some five thousand hospitals given over exclusively to the care of lepers; Matthew Paris estimated the European total for the three centuries as nineteen thousand, but most authorities believe this to be an overestimate. New hospitals were continually being opened, although many of them were relatively small. This is the period, too, of the establishment of numerous leper houses in England. Between 1200 and about 1400 some two hundred were opened. Ninety-five of these —the largest and most famous—were controlled by the monastic orders. Smaller houses, in villages and out-of-the-way places, were maintained by the local noble or the civil authorities. Seven of the larger houses—those at Canterbury and Northampton, for example—antedated the First Crusade.

The purpose of these houses was the segregation of the leper so that he might not transmit his disease, but that it was an inadequate and ineffective sort of segregation will appear in the next chapter. However well-intentioned and vigorous this and other measures were that at one time or another were undertaken for the suppression of leprosy, they were largely sterile because they were not based on any scientific knowledge either of the disease itself or of sanitation. The agency that was ultimately to be chiefly responsible (so far as we can now interpret our data) for the dying out of leprosy in Europe came from the outside, and was no part of any human plan. What laws could not avail to stamp out, what segregation could only somewhat reduce, what enforced celibacy combated ineffectually, was after three centuries brought about by the entry into Europe of another plague, the Black Death, a counter-irritant strong and swift in its application of relief measures.

Between 1300 and 1400 no fewer than fourteen plagues visited England, at six-year intervals, and the Black Death, last and most frightful, also swept the Continent. These, and the change in the people's diet that followed them, may colorably be credited with the substantial decrease in leprosy by the early 15th century. The total effect of this final pestilence is beyond our knowledge; what we do know of it is almost beyond comprehension or description. Contemporary popular imagination expressed it in prints that are familiar to us, showing a fearful, shadowy, sable-clad figure on a black horse roaming the countryside, or a giant striding along at dusk, his head towering high over the roofs, the scythe in his hand cutting down the shuddering creatures below him. The Black Death came to Europe from China, having started in that country in about 1333; following the great trade-routes of the time, it descended upon India, Persia, and Russia, and then from several directions entered western Europe. It was a violent disease; its victims died within twenty-four hours. When it was over, thousands of towns and villages had been completely wiped out, and the deserted roads were given over to the wild beasts of the forest. Exact mortality figures are not to be had, but it appears that Europe lost between a fourth and a third of its populations, and that nearly one half of the English people had perished. The clerical figures for England, which are fairly trustworthy, record more than twenty-five thousand deaths among the clergy. The city of Florence had a population of 130,000 before the plague; only 30,000 of these were alive afterward.

Precisely how this plague brought about the decline of leprosy has not been clearly established. But what is noteworthy—and quite certain—is that immediately after it died out there was a sudden and marked drop in the older disease; and this decline continued steadily until at last leprosy had almost vanished. That there was a causal relationship here seems unescapable. The Black Death struck first at the weak and sick and undernourished, and these classes were already leprosy's easiest prey. It is conceivable that the twenty-five percent of the European population who were lepers provided the Black Death with its earliest victims. But whether this is true or not, certainly there were far fewer lepers afterward than before.

Among the economic changes concurrent with the Black Death was a gradual improvement in diet and living conditions. With the introduction of vegetables into England there came a marked decrease in the consumption of salted meat and fish; black bread, too, was less used. And this advance in dietary helped further to reduce—just as we know it reduces today—the amount of leprosy. The decline appears to have started early in the 14th century, and a hundred years later leprosy had practically vanished on the Continent. In 1346 it was reported that there was not a single leper in London, and that many of the hospitals had been closed. By 1364 the large lazar house at Lincoln had but one inmate, and the same year discovered the fact that there were none at all in the largest hospital in Kent. By 1600 it was regarded as a rare disease, though France did not close her last lazar house until 1695. For a time, during the decline,

TOWERING CLIFFS NEAR THE LEPER SETTLEMENT.   THE WHITE
SPECKS IN THE DISTANCE ON THE RIGHT ARE THE BALDWIN HOME

there were a few localized outbreaks, mostly in seaports; the last section of England to be so visited was Cornwall.

By the time of the suppression of the monasteries by Henry VIII, the day of their services in watching over England's lepers had long passed. During eight hundred years the spiritual and social care of these most wretched of outcasts was assumed by the monastic orders, until at last there was no further need of their ministrations.

## CHAPTER II

### THE LEPER AND THE CHURCH

MEDIEVAL England has left records from which we may reconstruct with reasonable completeness the tragedy of the leper; and probably the details of his life there may be taken as representative of his social and religious status throughout Europe during the period when leprosy flourished. It is not a pretty story, this of humanity handicapped by ignorance and superstition and struggling with a tremendous social problem. Its background must be borne in mind: the prevailing belief that this disease was not like other human diseases but was rather a curse sent by God as punishment for sin, and that its victim must therefore be driven forth into the wilderness. The leper was spiritually as well as physically unclean. This attitude, together with the belief that the disease was infectious, goes far to justify the apparent harshness of the laws governing the leper's conduct, and explains, too, the regulations set up for the examination of suspects. For before a person could fairly be deprived of his normal status in the eyes of the Church and the State it must be established indubitably that he had contracted leprosy. The greatest care must be taken lest a healthy person be branded as a leper, and equally that no actual leper should be allowed to endanger his healthy neighbors. The prerequisite examination is therefore of interest.

As soon as a person was suspected he was told to stay in his house until he could be examined. He was then visited by a physician, with precise formality. First he was required to swear that he would answer truthfully all the questions that were put. Then followed a searching inquiry into his own history as well as that of his family. Had he ever touched a leper in the market-place? Had he ever slept with a leper? Had any member of his family ever been infected, or visited a leper house? Such questions point to the current belief that the disease was infectious and inheritable.

The suspect was then ordered to strip, and the color and sensitiveness of his skin were examined. He was pricked with knives to determine whether the sense of feeling had been lost. The physician next looked to see whether the eyebrows had thickened, whether the hair was going, whether the voice had harshened, whether there were ulcers on the limbs. This part of the examination might, instead, take place before the removal of the clothing. If results were positive there was no need to go further; but if they were negative, the examination proceeded. The body was carefully looked over for dark spots, for thickened joints. Invariably water was poured over the naked body to discover whether the skin was oily; for an oily skin was regarded as a mark of the disease. The blood and the urine were tested last.

Often it was not easy to decide whether the suspect really had leprosy. The physician was warned that he must make very certain, for a mistaken diagnosis might banish a perfectly healthy man from the world and deprive him of his goods and his family. If there was any doubt, or if the disease was not advanced, the person might be allowed to stay at home rather than go to a leper hospital. He might not associate with the healthy, nor leave his house, nor frequent public places; but would be supervised by a physician who could watch the progress of the disease. Thousands of mildly infected lepers lived all their lives in their own homes, especially rich folk or nobles or those who joined the Order of St. Lazarus. The poor man, on the other hand, when proved leprous was turned over to the ecclesiastical authorities, who read the leper mass over him and then either consigned him to a leper hospital or to one of the smaller shelters whose neglected inmates supported existence by begging. The suspect who was proved to be free from the disease was dismissed with the physician's certificate to that effect.

The next step, in the case of a proved leper who was not to be allowed to stay at home, was the notifying of the ecclesiastical authorities. The victim must remain indoors until the priest should come to take him to the church for the leper mass. The first part of the religious service of banishment took place at the leper's home. At some time during the morning (though certain manuscripts indicate that this service was held shortly after midnight) the priest left the church, preceded by a cross-bearer holding his gleaming symbol on high. Arrived at the house they knocked and entered. The leper met them by falling on his knees to hear the pronouncement. He was then reminded that his affliction was from the hand of God, a Divine punishment that could not be escaped. He must bear his sufferings meekly, remembering that after the shame and anguish of this world would come the ease and glory of the next. It might be, indeed, that he had been thus afflicted as an earnest of special bliss reserved for him in the future. A prayer followed, and the kneeling figure was sprinkled with holy water. The leper was then commanded to rise and accompany the priest to the church, where the leper mass was to be said.

Within the church there was always set up for this occasion a symbolic burial canopy, not far from the altar. It stood on four stakes and was covered with a black cloth. Under this the leper knelt, as a sign that he was no longer a living man. The burial mass was sung, and at its conclusion the priest threw a handful of earth over him or touched his shoulders with soil. If the leper elected to make his confession during the service, it must be a public confession, the priest standing some distance away from the penitent.

This burial ritual was identical in almost all of its details with that used at an actual funeral. No obituary was read, no laudatory address. Later on, a French bishop ordered that the use of earth be discontinued, but for many years before that time the form of the service was everywhere uniform. There was only one variation; in some places the leper was wrapped in a shroud at his home, and placed on a bier, which his family and friends followed as he was carried to the church for the requiem mass. In either form, however, the purpose of the service was to separate the leper from the rest of the world; when it was over, he had lost his civil, social, and religious rights.

Sometimes the service did not end with the reading of the mass. The leper might be taken out of the church into the burial-ground, where he found an open grave. In the variant form described above, it was here at the side of the grave that the earth was thrown on him, rather than inside the church. Another prayer would be read, and a psalm, the priest told him again to put his trust in God. He then heard the special duties he must now assume and the prohibitions that he must henceforth observe, and was given certain things to carry. He was warned that any infraction of the rules would bring punishment, death perhaps—real death this time. His clothes were taken from him, and the special leper garb donned. A wooden clapper or rattle was put into his hand, which he must always carry, sounding it before him as he went his way, to warn others of his approach. Since he must never touch anything with his hands, he was given gloves and a long staff with a small bucket attached to it; in this must be put all food and drink that he begged or bought.

The detailed prohibitions that were read to him were in many cases founded on laws established by the local lords, later by edicts of the king. The leper might never enter a church, convent, tavern, mill, or any other public place. He must never pass anyone without sounding his rattle when seven paces distant. If he came upon another unawares, he must sound his rattle and hurry past. He must not walk on narrow footpaths or on frequented roads, nor wash himself in the common springs and streams. When he must speak to a passerby, he was to take such a position that the wind might blow away from him. He must never touch a child, not even his own.

He was allowed to enter the towns on certain speci-fied days only—market days, as a rule. But on such occasions he must not eat with any healthy person, nor touch him. If he wished to buy wine or food he must not touch it with his hands but must indicate it with his staff. The seller might not hand his wares over directly, but must put them into the bucket held out at the end of the staff. The leper must not go out without his gloves, nor wear any dress except the special garb by which he was recognized. The reading of these rules concluded the service. It should be un-derstood, however, that not every leper went through these rites of formal separation from the world—there must have been cases innumerable that did not thus pass through the hands of the authorities.

But whatever his status in this respect, his civil position was clearly defined, increasingly so as the number of lepers grew larger and more and more laws were enacted regarding them. In certain districts, for instance, the leper was obliged to pay the death tax. All rights that he might have had in the common law courts were taken from him, and his property was at once divided among his heirs. He could not sue nor be brought to court, nor could he inherit or hold property. If he held public office at the time his disease was discovered, the office was void; nor could he ever afterward hold any religious, military, or civil position. In most cases he was not obliged to give tithes of the increase of his cattle or his garden. For in the eyes of both State and Church he was dead. Indeed, as late as Coke, the common law of England classed lepers with idiots and madmen.

His marital status was likewise annulled. For a husband who was a leper was dead; his wife was therefore a widow and might remarry, though she saw her leprous husband daily in the streets. On the Continent the laws under several reigns made leprosy a ground for divorce.

Once the leper had been cast out of human society his destiny was either the leper hospital or else—particularly if he were poor or friendless—the small, isolated cabin where he was to live henceforth. In this latter case his lot was wretched indeed. It must be remembered that although there were an immense number of hospitals of good size, systematically run and well endowed, these could hardly, in an age when a third of the population were lepers, care for all who had claims on their shelter. The consequence was that innumerable victims everywhere were gathered together in wretched little half-ruined huts outside the city gates or in the forests, depending for their support on the alms of the community. A medieval manuscript speaks of "leprous creatures dwelling in solitary huts by the water bank, permitted to seek the aid of passengers who went by in boats, from which alms were conveyed in floating boxes sent from the shore."

The charitable help extended to lepers had as its motive sometimes the idea mentioned above—that the leper's sufferings were a sign of God's special favor, a token of his future reward; for from this idea sprang the feeling that the leper was in a sense sacred and must be ministered to even by those in high places. Henry III of England endowed many leper hospitals. True, most of the land thus bestowed did not belong to him but was taken from his subjects; yet one must give him credit for not having seized it for himself. He even personally washed and dressed the lepers' sores. The Empress Matilda sold her bed and gave the proceeds to the lepers.

But this attitude seems to have been sporadic and exceptional. Nothing is more certain than that the dominating feeling everywhere and at all periods was an intense horror and fear on the part of those who had not yet been attacked by the disease. That this terror occasionally broke forth into active persecution was only natural. Henry II of England, in a panic following his discovery that he himself had fallen victim to the plague, threatened to burn every leper in the land—which at the time would have meant at least a fourth of his subjects.

The ultimate purpose of laws and examinations alike found its concrete expression in the leper hospital. We must beware, however, of reading into this term our modern conception of a hospital. The medieval institution was maintained not for the healing of the sick but for the shelter of poor outcasts and—in the case of lepers—for the protection of the well outside its doors. Within, the leper hospital was not unlike a prison, its theory being the complete segregation of its inmates.

It is natural, considering the dominating position of the medieval Church, that she should have been the agency that first assumed the care of the lepers. But the marked increase in the number of European leper hospitals after the Crusades was due rather to a special organization within her fold, the Order of St. Lazarus. For many years before the Crusades—indeed ever since Helena, the mother of Constantine, had reported her discovery of the true Cross—Jerusalem had been the goal of pilgrims. As the first millennium after Christ drew to its close pilgrimages had become a special form of penance. For minor sins a journey to a nearby shrine was considered sufficient; but the supreme penance for heinous crimes was the long and painful pilgrimage to the Holy City itself. There were six of these in the 8th century, but by the 11th, just before the First Crusade, the number had increased to more than a hundred, each of them composed of hundreds of persons.

The pilgrims often arrived at Jerusalem stricken with fevers acquired during their journeys. To care for these there had been established hospitals under the control of certain religious orders. In a sense they were medical hospitals, for they aimed at curing their patients. The order whose seal showed a sick man lying on a cot was to be known as the Knights of St. John at a later period when it had become a semi-military order whose duty it was to protect the Holy Land from the infidel.

The most famous of these special orders was the Knights of St. Lazarus, a religious and military society formed in order that the knights and nobles among the Crusaders should not be deprived of their honors when they contracted leprosy. This order was established in the middle of the 12th century at Jerusalem, where it opened a leper hospital, and gradually it made its way throughout the whole of Europe. The knights in the order supervised the leper hospitals and cared for the needs of the inmates. During the early period of its existence the Order was bound to elect a leper as Grand Master, but under Pope Innocent IV this rule was abolished.

History presents no finer picture of devotion and service to humanity than the Knights of St. Lazarus. All of them were members of the ruling classes who had been so unfortunate as to contract leprosy. As the plague swept through Europe their responsibilities grew heavier and more extensive. Presently King Louis of France—Saint Louis—brought twelve of the knights to France so that they might instruct others in the management of leper hospitals. Ultimately these knights had the nominal supervision of all the French lazar houses, their head being subject to the master of the Order's lazar house in Jerusalem. As leprosy began to disappear, the need for the Order lessened, and at last it was dissolved as having lost its reason for existence.

In England the chief leper hospitals were unevenly distributed, the majority being located in the eastern and southern coast counties—their natural place, since the largest centers of population were near the sea. Thus Norfolk at one time had seventeen houses of the first rank, and Kent nine. Most of these larger leper houses were opened during the 12th century, the period of the greatest increase of the disease in England. Sherburne Hospital, near Durham, was one of the wealthiest and most extensive, and it was always filled.

The best-known of the English houses and most of the thousands on the Continent were religious institutions controlled by ecclesiastical authority. In many cases their endowments were large enough to provide adequate incomes. Commonly these endowments were in land; for land, with its revenue from rents and tithes, provided the only certainly permanent income. The gifts took various forms. One legacy—to the Dover hospital—bequeathed one hundred acres, including a fishpond. Henry III in one of his bursts of vicarious generosity presented to St. John's Hospital at Oxford the garden belonging to the Jews of that town. Mills were often given, even churches sometimes. Instead of real property the hospitals occasionally received gifts of other kinds. Odo Dammartin gave one of them a windmill, books, silver cups, and seven cows. Henry III, again presenting property not his own, gave the Shrewsbury hospital one horseload of wood a day from Lynwood Forest. St. Thomas at Southwick had one annuity of £343—equal to some $4000 in our money today; though money was a rarity and was seldom given. But the privileges often conferred on the hospitals were valuable.

Not all of the leper houses, however, were specially endowed. The larger ones, established by the great monasteries, shared in the immense wealth that had been amassed by these institutions. The Benedictines particularly had acquired both power and riches for the monasteries of their order, which served not only as religious houses but also as gathering places for travelers of every sort. The rule of the Order commanded that "all guests who come shall be received as though they were Christ." No one was turned away —princes, commoners, and beggars alike found hospitality in the guest house; and the abbot was bound by his oath to seat guests at his own table.

The monasteries, when they took over the task of caring for the lepers, adopted various methods of meeting this fresh burden on their funds. Some of the larger establishments financed the new undertaking from their plentiful incomes; others made rules requiring entrants to pay fees for their care. In some cases the leper, at the conclusion of the special mass, paid a death tax just as his estate would have done if he had really died. Other hospitals required him to make over his estate to them on admission. Finally, many of the hospitals were supported either by tolls collected at the markets or by general taxes laid on the fairs and on the public at large.

Since these markets were held weekly, in some places semi-weekly, and since all the local buying and selling of every sort of commodity was concentrated in them, the tolls collected on the goods must have represented a considerable source of income for the leper hospitals. The Harleian Manuscript records the details of a market toll taken "from everything that was carried to the Chester market." The tolls were collected at the city gates when the wares were carried in. For example, from every horse-drawn load of the fruit of trees there was taken one double handful. From each package of earthenware one piece went to the leper hospital; from sacks of salt one handful; and from sacks of malt and oats two handfuls. From each cartload of cheeses one was taken; and from every pannier of fish five went to the hospital.

Other localities had rules similar to those cited for Chester. One bishop granted toll of all corn and bread sold in the town markets of his diocese. At Shrewsbury two handfuls of every sack of corn brought

to market went to the hospital. Some of the customs
were curious. The rule that tainted salmon and pork
found in any market must be condemned and then
sent to the lazar house is matched by another to the
effect that "if a wounded or dead beast be found in the
forest, it must be sent to the nearest leper home." In
Scotland, where leprosy made its appearance after it
had begun to decline in England, the flesh of diseased
animals that could not be sold in the public markets
was often sent to the leper houses for their inmates.
A Scottish act of Parliament in 1386 tells us in quaint
language that "if any man bring to the market corrupt
swine or salmond to be sauld, they sall be taken by the
bailie without any question and sent to the leper folk;
and if there be no leper folk, they sall be destoryed."

Funds were derived also from certain of the large
fairs. Every English town and village had an annual
fair, the larger ones being held by towns at some distance from the coast, and under grants either from the
local lord or from the king. The lord who gave the
grant built the booths and policed the fair, receiving
rent and toll from all who attended. Local and neigh-
boring trade was forbidden, and the merchants came
from all over Europe. There were a few fairs whose
entire proceeds went to the support of the lepers; of
these the most famous was that held at Stourbridge
under a grant from King John. It lasted for two
weeks, and all of its takings went to the leper hospital
at Cambridge. People came from all parts of England
to buy the foreign merchants' wares, which seem

chiefly to have been hops, wool, hardware, and leather goods, with one day given up to the sale of horses. The large revenue was sufficient to enable the Cambridge hospital to care for all the lepers within its walls.

Finally, the leper hospitals derived income from public alms collected on stated days from the citizens. This appears to have been a general tax, for special proctors were appointed to collect the offerings. An amusing light on one immutable trait of mankind is thrown by the records describing an abuse that grew out of this custom: it seems that unauthorized persons —beggars, in fact—took to going about claiming to be these tax-collectors and taking in the alms, so that eventually a special identifying garb and badge had to be provided for the proctors, to make sure that the money gathered reached the proper authorities.

From the regulations of these houses we gather a picture of a life that was not entirely uncomfortable or unhappy. Each leper was given daily a loaf of bread and a gallon of ale. This latter does not seem so extravagant when we read that every monk in the monastery received the same amount daily, and that at another house each inmate had fourteen gallons given him at Christmas time. Three times a week there was shared between each two lepers a stated quantity of meat; if flesh was not to be had (we have said that it was rarely used), or if the meal was of fish, then cheese and butter were added during four days. Each leper received a quantity of bean meal every day

The Old Man of
Molokai Greets his
very dear friend
Hon. W. O. Smith

Ash Wednesday
1920.

"THE OLD MAN OF MOLOKAI"

except Sunday. The food was cooked in a common kitchen, and a cook was provided, with fuel and utensils for cooking. On special festival days the food allowance was greatly increased. In one hospital fire and candles were provided for all lepers. There was a clothing allowance, too—"three yards of woolen cloth, white or russet, six yards of linen, and six of canvas." A tailor was brought into the house to cut and fit and sew the garments. On cold days during the damp winter months each inmate had four basketfuls of peat. Christmas brought a special celebration, with extra food and a gift of five shillings in money for each inmate; and four large Yule logs were burned in the great fireplace.

Obviously in such an institution it was not impossible for the leper to live an indolent and—apart from the inescapable horrors of his disease—fairly comfortable life. His most crying need, of course, was medical attention; and this he did not get. The physician might be meticulously painstaking in the examination of the suspect, but once having diagnosed leprosy his care went no farther. It was not only that in those days the doctors did not know of any cure or even of any palliation for the disease; it was that, in view of its Divine origin as a judgment on the sinner, any attempt at a cure would have constituted a contravention of the will of God. Some hospitals had nurses to dress the patients' sores, but the common idea was that what was called for was not medical treatment but penance. If any cure was to be hoped for, it must come from God.

We should be misinterpreting the spirit of the age if we concluded that the solemn rite of the leper mass was in any sense excommunication. True, the leper might not enter a church or a convent; he could no longer attend mass in an ordinary church; he could not marry. But the Church never took the position that he had ceased to be a part of it or had been placed outside of its authority. The ritual was a practical measure through which the diseased individual was separated from society; but he was not excommunicate. It may be noted that up to the 8th century the leper, because he was presumed dead, was not allowed to receive the Eucharist; but Gregory II readmitted lepers to the sacrament.

Many hospitals had chaplains whose duty it was to read the office to the lepers. In the larger ones there were priests and brothers who assisted in the services, which the inmates were required to attend. Hubert, Archbishop of Canterbury, ruled in 1200 that whenever there were enough lepers in one place they might build a church and have a churchyard for their own use, and thus be able to attend daily mass. There were several instances of such small leper churches, though in most places there were no funds to build them. As for the churches in which the public worshiped—which lepers might not enter—there is a tradition that the narrow openings in the walls, called hagioscopes, were for the use of lepers outside, who might thus look within and see the elevation of the

Host. This, however, is not established, though in popular speech these odd openings have long been called leper windows.

The rules of conduct imposed on the entrant into a leper hospital were as clearly specified as were those dictated by the priest after the leper mass. Some were conditions laid down before he was admitted, as for instance the requirement made by one hospital that each leper on entering must pay £5 into the treasury and also bring with him a purse with a penny in it and a pot to cook his meat in. For the most part, however, no fee was demanded. But once inside he encountered a rigid discipline. At every turn he was reminded that he was not like other men, that he must humble himself continually before others who had not been so afflicted. If he had been a married man he must take a vow of chastity. His clothes were taken from him and burnt—if this had not already been done —and he was given "clothing suitable for his infirmities." This consisted of an upper tunic of russet cloth, a black hood, and flat shoes with upper leathers above the ankles.

The rules in some of the monasteries, like some of the civil rules, seem very cruel. In 1283 Berwick-on-the-Tweed passed a law that any leper entering the town should have his clothes burnt and be driven out into the fields naked. In Marseilles at the same period it was ordered that any leper refusing to enter a hospital should be burnt alive. When leprosy reached Scotland and a large hospital was built in Edinburgh, the law provided that no leper could go outside the building after dusk, nor would its doors be opened then; the penalty for disobedience was death. To impress this further on the inmates a gallows was erected at the door of the hospital, and offenders were put to death at once. In 1321 two lepers who fled from the house at Schenalle were arrested, flogged, and then burnt.

All such laws were the expression of the theory of segregation that underlay the leper hospitals. But in England this segregation seems never to have been strict. Many a record shows how half-hearted it was. Though the laws forbade the leper to be seen in certain places, yet he never was completely cut off from the world. He was allowed to leave the hospital and roam the highways. Though provided with food and lodging he was expected to go out and beg, adding to his food by buying at the markets. Many of the houses were situated at the city gates, and the lepers were forbidden to pass through the walls; yet they could be seen at any time of day clustered near the gates and lifting up their voices for alms. Nor does there seem to have been any attempt to debar healthy friends and relatives from visiting the hospitals. Of all the rules that have come down to us none touches on this matter of visitors except to prescribe the hour when outsiders must depart and leave the leper to himself. They might crowd into the hospital to visit, share the lepers' food; only, when the gates were closed at nightfall they must go.

The penalties for infraction of these rather nominal regulations seem to have been quite illogical in some places, even topsy-turvy. The hospital of St. Julian, at St. Albans, expelled a leper if he remained outside the house for a single night; in another, on the third infraction of the rules the inmate was turned out and sent forth to live among his fellows again.

Then, rather suddenly, leprosy began to decline. By 1346 there was not, for example, a single leper left in London. The ancient laws were still in existence but had fallen into disuse, and the leper mass had joined other obsolete rituals. In France the decline was somewhat slower; it was early in the 16th century that Francis I ordered the privileges of the leper houses revised and the number of true lepers determined. Since the investigation proved that the lepers were by this time few, hundreds of hospitals were closed, and the funds—now far too large for the need—were redistributed. A century later, Louis XIV abolished the remaining hospitals as being no longer needed, and their property was given to the Carmelites. One hospital only was allowed to survive, the last of more than two thousand.

As the plague decreased in England it attacked Scotland, where it lingered until the middle of the 18th century. Meanwhile, what had been going on in England for several hundred years was repeated north of the Tweed: leper hospitals were established and segregating laws were passed. In 1742 Scotland held a special day of celebration marking the final disappearance of leprosy within its borders. Though a few sufferers still remained, the plague as a plague had ceased.

One episode of the declining stages of leprosy in England has an amusing side for city-dwellers among us today. There seems to have been a vague attempt made to identify causes, or predisposing conditions, and when soft coal was first introduced, its use was forbidden in both London and Southwick on the ground that the smoke was responsible for spreading leprosy!

This story of the spread and sudden decline of leprosy in England and Europe is one of the most interesting and perplexing chapters in medical history. Why the disease took its violent upward leap is a question that perhaps will never be satisfactorily answered. Even more puzzling is the greater mystery of its sudden check and rapid decline. One must remember that of the hundreds of thousands who suffered and died, not one was cured. The Church might pronounce the leper dead in the eyes of man, the State might pass laws which separated him from human society, but neither Church nor State could cure him. Centuries were to pass before medical science would announce that the first leper had been cured.

# CHAPTER III

## FROM OCEAN TO OCEAN

THE discovery of America and the early voyages of Spanish and Portuguese explorers led to an exchange between the Old World and the New whose results were to be far-reaching. All authorities agree that until this time there had been no leprosy in America. The aboriginal Indians of both South and North America knew nothing of the disease before the white race landed among them. It was Columbus's sailors who brought leprosy in, and in exchange they carried back to Europe that other equally terrible plague, syphilis.

That this was the source of syphilis in Europe is believed by nearly all authorities, though there are some who assert that no unquestionably pre-Columbian syphilitic bones have ever been discovered in either of the Americas, and that the disease existed only in Haiti. This latter view remains to be proved. Bloch, whose "Der Ursprung der Syphilis" is the most extensive work on the subject, says that syphilis came to Europe from Haiti, having been brought to Spain by Columbus's sailors, and spread like a flame to Italy, where the soldiers of Charles VIII of France contracted it in 1494. The very severity of the disease and its infectious sweep through the whole of Europe after 1492 prove it to have been a new plague that found a fresh, untouched soil on which to grow.

The presence of syphilis in medieval Europe complicates any research into the problem of contemporary leprosy. The two diseases are somewhat alike, and they were often confused by the physicians of the time. Historically, syphilis followed the same course as leprosy, spreading with lightning rapidity over Europe and soon completely overshadowing the older plague, which was then dying out.

Just where and when the first leper hospital was established in the New World is doubtful. Diaz, in his vivid description of the conquest of Mexico by Cortes, mentions that the Spanish general was forced to open a hospital for his sick soldiers, and there is slight evidence that this was a leper hospital, for among the nearly seven hundred men who made up his army there were some lepers. Yet it is open to question whether a few leprous soldiers could so suddenly and so gravely infect others that a hospital would be required for this one disease exclusively. It is certain that a hospital was opened, but it was more probably for the syphilitic, since the army had only just come into contact with this new disease, and syphilis attacked them rapidly and violently; moreover the vague description of their ailment might apply as well to syphilis as to leprosy.

However this may have been, there is no doubt about the hospital that was established at Cartagena

less than fifty years after the discovery of America.
This seacoast city of Colombia was founded in 1533
by Pedro de Heredia, and from the beginning was a
large and flourishing town.  Its first inhabitants were
explorers, freebooters, and pirates, and many of the
most familiar and bloodcurdling adventures on the
Spanish Main in the 16th century center around
Cartagena.  Its position on the coast, its proximity to
the wealth of Mexico and Peru, and its unusually fine
harbor made it for almost a hundred years the most
important city in the New World.  Here was the first
slave market in the Americas, where natives taken
captive by the Spanish were sold into slavery; their
association with the men from the ships—sailors and
soldiers already infected with leprosy—carried the
scourge to other natives.  The hospital here—the first
for which we have documentary proof—had at one
time more than a hundred inmates and was the largest
in the new settlements.  What appears to have been
the second was founded in Lima, Peru, in 1535, thirty
years after Pizarro established the city.

During the two centuries following the coming of
the Spanish, leprosy crept slowly through South
America, until today it is found in all parts of that
continent.  But for some reason—perhaps because communication was difficult, or because the northern
continent was sparsely settled—it never gained a foothold in North America.  Even now it is among our
rarest diseases, the Public Health Service figures for
January 2, 1931, showing about 1,100 cases reported

for the entire country.

When it did enter what is now the United States it did so from an unexpected direction: not from the South but from the North, though it appeared first in New Orleans. (The story that there were a few cases among the Spanish settlers in Florida is not supported by good evidence.) The plague was sent down to Louisiana by the same historical event that gave us Longfellow's *Evangeline*—the expulsion by the British of the French settlers in Acadia and New Brunswick in the 18th century. It is said—though we must accept the statement guardedly—that leprosy came into New Brunswick through the wreck of a French vessel on the coast; that there were three Orientals in the crew, and that these had died of leprosy only three days before the shipwreck; that their clothes were distributed among several of the families that had helped in the rescue—and that it was this clothing that was responsible for infecting the French settlers. If this is so, then the French on being driven forth and going far south to their fellow-countrymen in Louisiana carried the disease with them. And it is a fact that until the Acadians came to New Orleans there was no leprosy in that city; and that New Orleans became the center of leprosy in this country and that our first leper hospital was established there in 1778.

It is when we turn our attention to the island possessions of our country that we meet the problem in its gravest aspect. Leprosy was a familiar epidemic in what we now call the Hawaiian Islands many years

before these came into the possession of the United
States, although it had not been known there until the
Europeans came exploring and colonizing.   Just when
it was introduced there is disputed.   In 1798 the North
Pacific whaling fleet began to visit the Islands, and it
is said that the mixed crews of Negroes, Portuguese,
and Chinese brought the disease in.   The Hawaiian
natives themselves began in 1810 to export sandal-
wood to China and thus came into contact with the
lepers of that country.   Around 1833 several missionaries reported that the natives were afflicted with
sores and ulcers; though this may mean that they had
been infected with syphilis by the visiting whaling
fleets.   And in 1840 a captain of the Royal Guard of
the palace was thought to have contracted leprosy.
But, however uncertain the date of the introduction
of this disease, there is no doubt about the date when
it was publicly recognized.   In April, 1863, a surgeon
of Queen's Hospital, Honolulu, called the attention of
the Government to the fact that leprosy was rapidly
spreading among the Hawaiians.   In one small village
fifty cases had been observed, and he said that he had
no doubt that parallel conditions existed in other
places.   This first public recognition of the existence
of leprosy in the Islands led to immediate investigation
and action.

The character and the customs of the Hawaiians
offered fertile soil for the spread of the plague.
Happy-go-lucky and sociable in a high degree, they
facilitated it by their hospitality and sexual com-

munism. Their habits of kissing and of nose-rubbing; their method of preparing the native drink *aui*—by masticating leaves; their custom of eating from the same dish and of smoking the same pipe; the fact that sick and well exchanged clothing—all these encouraged the spread of leprosy. It increased slowly at first, and they seemed to have no fear of it, nor would they take any precautions. It presently gained a firm foothold, and played havoc throughout the Islands as nowhere else in the world.

By 1864 the plague had assumed terrible proportions, though, owing to the communal life of the islanders, it was impossible to collect trustworthy figures showing its actual extent. The fact that the natives themselves would take no precautions against infection led the Hawaiian legislature in 1865 to pass an act "to prevent the further spread of leprosy by segregating the afflicted." The passage of this act was accompanied by bitter controversy, during which all that was then known about the disease was brought forth. The only possible remedy seemed to be segregation, for every authority believed leprosy to be infectious, and no cure was known. It was the white population that forced the bill through, not the Hawaiians themselves; and the act was to become very unpopular and generally evaded.

Under this act as passed on January 3, 1865, plans were made for a hospital, and land was bought for a leper colony. The first site chosen was the Palolo valley on the Island of Oahu. Now this was the chief

Island of the group and was thickly populated.  But
it was recognized that any segregation must involve isolation—the lepers must be deprived of any possible
contact with the healthy outside world; and so, when
the people of Oahu heard of the proposal to set a leper
colony down in their midst they protested vigorously,
and this idea was abandoned.  Forthwith a second site
was determined on, whose name was to become world-
famous.

Of the eight principal Islands that make up the
group known as the Territory of Hawaii, Molokai is
fifth in size, covering some 261 square miles.  It is
almost thirty-eight miles long and has a width of about
seven miles.  East and west across the Island runs an
irregular ridge of high mountains, in some places
forming great cliffs against whose base the sea beats.
Elsewhere the cliffs run back from the water, with
gullies, gulches, and plains reaching inland.  On the
northern side there is but one projection of land—a
projection comprising nearly 6,350 acres, three miles
wide and two and a half deep.  Behind it and enclosing it on two sides are steep, perpendicular cliffs from
two to four thousand feet high, impassable except
through an old and dangerous trail over the mountains.  The latter are of volcanic origin; there is an
extinct crater on the Island.  This tongue of land,
therefore, possesses natural isolation in an unusual
degree, the mountains inland forming an almost impassable barrier on that side, and on the other the sea,
with Honolulu fifty-two miles away.  But it offers

some of the most beautiful scenery in the world and
has a climate far finer than that of Honolulu.

It was this projection of land that was the second
choice for the leper colony. Nothing could be said
against a spot offering the dual advantages of perfect
isolation and perfect climate. The Island itself was
sparsely settled; the high mountains and the absence
of any harbor had discouraged settlers. Once the
lepers were sent there, escape would be impossible;
this was evidently the place in which to segregate them.

Meanwhile there had been an effort to start a hospital at Kalihi near Honolulu, and it was opened in
November, 1865. Here any persons suspected of leprosy were to be examined, retained, and perhaps
treated; though the treatment was a farce. This, the
first hospital in the Islands, proved useful far more for
examination than for segregation. What was wanted
was real isolation. Moreover there were loud objections to having the hospital so near to the largest city
on the Islands. It was therefore decided to make the
hospital exclusively a place for examination, and to
establish the proposed leper colony elsewhere; and
Molokai was chosen.

The first settlement was made on the eastern side
of the projection of land, at Kalawao—an exposed spot
swept by the trade-winds and backed by towering
cliffs, not far from the valley of Waikolu, which was
noted for its rich soil and abundant rainfall. In
choosing this site the officials made one of the most
egregious of all the errors that were to characterize

their conduct of the colony.

Human intentions are perhaps more often good than evil, but the best intentions may have sorry results if their authors are unacquainted with what has been called "the moral obligation to be intelligent." The Waikolu valley was seen to be fertile; crops could be grown with little trouble. Therefore put the lepers there—they will cultivate the soil and thus become self-supporting: that was the general idea. What seems not to have entered the heads of the authorities is that the lepers were sick people, suffering from a hideous disease that would grow progressively worse and for which there was no cure; that men and women whose fingers, hands, and toes were rotting off could hardly support themselves by tilling the soil. Here was an absurdity that was to bear bitter fruit before this site was abandoned—an absurdity that nevertheless was repeated in the next experiment. Presently it became apparent that the rich soil was not being cultivated, and that the dampness of the deep valley made it an impossible place for sick persons.

More land was then obtained, a large part of the holdings in other sections of the peninsula being taken over. Buildings were started, and the removal of the lepers to this new district began. In 1866 there were 141 taken to the Island.

This removal was not effected without difficulty and even bloodshed. From the very first the segregation law was unpopular except among the whites. The natives considered it not only unjust but cruel; they

were not afraid of leprosy, they did not mind being
infected—to this day a healthy Hawaiian will eat,
drink, and sleep with a leper, and even marry one
without any fear.  But they could not understand nor
accept the idea of separation from their friends and
condemnation to what was really life imprisonment.
So after the law was passed, families took to hiding in
the forest those of their number who were infected,
or they sent them into the mountains.  Bring them to
the hospital they would not.  The act consequently
fell into abeyance, largely because it was not enforced;
and, though the disease was known to be increasing,
during a period of some years only thirty lepers were
sent to the colony.

In 1873, with the coming of a new king who was in
sympathy with the segregation law, the authorities
revived their zeal.  Officials were given special police
powers under which they might hunt down the suspects and through the courts effect the segregation of
all identified as lepers.  This led to open rebellion.
Hundreds of lepers were hidden in caves and huts
deep within the forests, and several shooting affairs
between the officials and the hunted led to the fear
that only military measures could enforce the law.
Then certain episodes occurred that changed this
aspect of the situation.

There had been a feeling among the natives that
the segregation law was to be applied only to them,
only to the poor and uninfluential and defenseless.
But the new king ordered it enforced regardless of the

THE LEPER SETTLEMENT AT MOLOKAI

leper's rank or wealth; the royal family itself would not be exempted. Then a cousin of the Queen was discovered to be a leper and was at once sent to the colony. This started a favorable reaction that was increased by an even more sensational happening. There was in Honolulu a prominent half-white lawyer, well known in the Islands. One day he found that he had leprosy, and saw a chance to set an example to the natives. He asked publicly for an examination, got it, was pronounced leprous, and was sent to Molokai. This had a marked effect in reducing the general fear and resentment, and within a year afterward 500 lepers were isolated.

During the first eighteen years of the colony 3000 persons were received, including not only natives but also representatives of many other races of the world; more than 2000 died, and the rest suffered indescribably. For here too the unintelligent plans of the authorities had been put into effect with the results that might have been anticipated. If ever there was a hell on earth it was this "self-supporting" leper colony. The Government appears to have believed that the idea was practicable; and certainly, at least, it made the new experiment a cheap one and saved public money to buy the Island, transfer the lepers, and then let them shift for themselves cut off entirely from the world. A few grass huts were put up for the newcomers; not much else, except to provide—for more than 200 persons—a few heifers, two pairs of oxen, and some horses. Even the supply of food fur-

nished was meager, owing to the absurd expectation
that the lepers in less advanced stages would be able
to provide food for their worse-afflicted fellows.

The consequence? Within six months the once rich
and fertile fields were overgrown with high grass and
weeds. The lepers who had the disease less badly—
instead of helping the others—had taken possession of
all the supplies, had eaten the entire stock of food in
a few weeks, and had refused to replant anything.
They even took from the helpless and dying what
clothing had been provided, and the food that the
superintendent had distributed among those who were
unable to work at all. At the end of this period the
superintendent, a Frenchman named Leparat, wrote
to the Board at Honolulu that supplies were exhausted
and that it would be impossible for the lepers to main-
tain life on what crops they themselves could raise.

There were other difficulties, too. It seemed impossible to keep order. Near the colony on the
peninsula there lived a few old settlers whose land for
some reason had not been bought by the Government.
These stayed on, and—since they were not subject to
the rules of the settlement—did as they pleased; and
their influence on the lepers was distinctly corrupting.
Drunkenness, theft, sexual license, and rioting broke
out. Why not? Here was a group of people sent away
to die, and they realized it. Only a few managed to
break away and escape from the Island. The rest,
though they would not plant crops, did brew the
native beer, which, being made from the root of a wild

plant, was easy to produce; and soon there was no
semblance of order. The condition of those in the
last stages of the disease was unspeakably pitiable;
they lay on grass mats in half-ruined huts without
medical care or attention of any sort; for there were
no hospital facilities provided for more than a year
after they came. Every member of the colony was
steadily growing weaker. There was not even an
adequate water-supply; all they had was carried to the
settlement from some thousand yards away.

In 1867 the first superintendent resigned, and a
Mr. and Mrs. Walsh took his place. Walsh was to act
as schoolmaster for the leper children, and also as
magistrate; his wife was to nurse. In the colony were
a number of men whose wives were lepers and who
had come into exile with them; these Walsh made
constables. For their services they were given permission to stay on the Island, to live with their wives,
and to receive the same quantity of clothes and ra-
tions that was issued to the lepers. It is to be noted
that by this time the Hawaiian Government had re-
linquished the "self-supporting" idea and was pro-
viding supplies; in other respects, too, an effort was
being made to improve conditions in the colony.

Then Walsh died, and his wife was appointed in his
place, with a retired sea-captain for assistant. It was
not a happy appointment. The man and the woman
could not agree; and what was worse, neither one
could speak the native language. They passed rules
that were ignored, and the disorder increased.

Eventually there was a rebellion among the colonists, which invited harsh measures from the authorities. Its ringleaders were punished and both Mrs. Walsh and the sea-captain were dismissed. Their successor was a captain in the Hawaiian Royal Guard, named Kahoohuli, himself a leper. Though he managed within a few weeks to restore order, he found it impossible to bring about any real improvement in living conditions.

A new king presently came to the throne, and a new Board of Health was appointed; and conditions began slowly to get better. The first act of the new Board, however, raised an outcry: non-lepers were no longer to be allowed to go to the colony. Though the supply of food was increased, it was still insufficient. But the problem of the water-supply was met more satisfactorily, water-pipes being laid from a spring below the mountains and brought down to the hospital. True, the pipes were small, and there was sometimes no water; but the taps that had been placed at close intervals saved the lepers that former long, weary journey. A doctor was put into the hospital, and, though the supply of medicines was inadequate, some effort was made to treat the lepers who were most desperately ill.

Yet even after these improvements were effected, the lepers' situation remained tragic. Take their housing, for instance. The huts were small, makeshift affairs of grass or branches or sugarcane leaves, with no ventilation. The wind often blew them to the ground or destroyed them entirely. Some of the colonists went up the valleys to live by themselves in the shade of the high cliffs, where they cut down trees to make huts, or built rude shelters from the branches of the castor-oil trees. The many who had open sores on their feet could not get about; and these and others in all stages of the putrescent disease lay about in the tiny, fetid huts. Scores who had reached the final stage were dying alone, their shelters filled with the odor of their open ulcers. Filth lay thick everywhere, for there was scant attention given to hygiene. In the colony's early days, when a leper died the body was wrapped in a cloth and thrown into a grave. But these graves were barely under the surface of the ground, and scavenger dogs and wild pigs pawed them open, exposing the bones. The authorities later made an allowance of $2 apiece for coffins; but the lepers had to make their own coffins, and they found the $2 hard to collect. When coffins were used, moreover, the ground was so rocky that it was easier to pile them one above the other, three or four deep, covered by a few inches of soil.

There was never enough food, the allowance for clothing did not clothe them adequately, and there was nothing to do. Those in the first stages of the disease —a stage that often runs a mild course for years—found time lying heavy on their hands; so they played cards, danced the *hula,* and drank fermented *ki* or home-made root beer. The local authorities tried to suppress the brewing of this highly intoxicating liquor but were unsuccessful. Add together a morbid and fatalistic mental condition, idleness, the sense of being neglected, and unlimited quantities of crude home-brew—and you get utter demoralization. That was Molokai in the early '70's.

But the picture is not complete without further details. The number of lepers increased yearly; so did the character and variety of their needs. Yet a thrifty government applied only inadequate funds to meeting these needs, trusting still to the ability of the lepers to shift for themselves. In the year 1868, even after the hospital had been opened at Kalihi (Honolulu), the total expenditure on both hospital and settlement was only $24,803.60. As late as 1885 only $54,000 was spent on the colony in a year. Some improvement had been effected in the matter of clothing appropriations after the first years, but even as late as 1873 the amount assigned to each person was only $6 a year, and this was not in cash but in the form of an order on the colony store for goods. As for food, they were each now given five pounds of meat a week, or three pounds of salmon; with twenty-one pounds of *paiai* (native food) or ten of rice a month, and seven pounds of bread and five of salt. Wishing to encourage labor among those who were capable of it, the authorities ordered that any who were willing to cultivate the fields should receive in cash the equivalent of their food allowance.

But these provisions for clothing and food did not materially lighten the atmosphere of desperate neglect in which the lepers were allowed to live during the early period. For many years there were no physicians or trained nurses resident on the Island. A hospital there was, of sorts—a small one built in 1867 for the more advanced cases, but incapable of caring even for these properly. For years the "beds" here were only grass mats, and many of the patients had to lie on the bare floor without even this comfort. The nurses were untrained volunteers from among the colony's non-lepers. Even as late as 1873, the year of Father Damien's arrival, the hospital was in charge of a layman. This man, a Mr. Williamson, was a white and himself a leper, who had been a helper in the Kalihi hospital and so had picked up some practical knowledge of medicine. On being exiled to the colony he was put in charge of its hospital, having the care of all the patients and—later—assisted on the outside by Father Damien. For some time the Kalihi hospital sent doctors to the Island periodically to treat the lepers; but the latter refused the treatment, preferring the unscientific attentions of their fellow-sufferers and complaining that the doctors' visits were so short and hurried that little benefit was gained from them. Later the Government opened a large hospital at the base of the cliffs; but the lepers persisted in their refusal of treatment, and the hospital was closed. The situation seems to have been that men who were themselves dying by inches buried those who had died, and sick folk who were barely able to walk took care of others whose limbs were so rotted that they could no longer move.

These conditions were what Father Damien found when he came in 1873. What they were in 1874 he describes in a report that he wrote for the Board of Health in 1886. The lepers were still living in small, damp huts made from branches or reed-stalks, open to the wind and the rain. Practically all of them were lying helpless on their straw mats, covered with sores and unable to move about. The food they were allowed barely kept them from starvation, and it had no variety. They were huddled together with no distinction of sex, age, race, or degree of illness, the fresh cases sheltered by the same roof that covered the dying. The sick had no help, and the medical man visited the colony only once a month.

It is not easy to be patient when one thinks of the authorities responsible for such a situation. True, leprosy might be a relatively new problem in the Islands, and certainly the Government did not know —any more than anybody else did—how long the period of infection was or how to treat the disease after it had got started. They chose for the site of the colony the most fertile valley in the Islands, with an ideal climate. But, having learned after a six months' trial that the lepers could not be counted on to support themselves, or even to contribute anything considerable to their own support, why did the Government not profit by the lesson? Why keep on with a plan that had been proved a failure?

In the beginning, as we have said, 141 lepers went to the colony during the year 1866; by 1873 there were

749 persons there, the majority of them infected.
Lepers were originally allowed to take their husbands
or their wives with them, or even relatives who might
care for them; at one time during the early years the
number of healthy persons living in the settlement
was almost a fifth of its total population.  But in 1873
this privilege was withdrawn; not only were the well
members of the family not allowed to live on the
Island—they were not even allowed to visit it.  None
the less, stories telling of these conditions began to
reach the larger Islands, and the old feeling of bitter
resentment was once again aroused.  The hiding of
lepers by their family and friends continued.  The
agitation crept into the newspapers, and the suggestion
was made that the King ought to visit Molokai and
see the settlement for himself.  There was a renewed
effort to segregate known lepers strictly, with no class
distinctions.

It was at this time that *Nuhou,* a Honolulu newspaper, published on April 15, 1873, an editorial whose
suggestion was to bear valuable fruit: "If a noble
Christian preacher, priest, or sister should be inspired
to go and sacrifice a life to console these poor wretches,
that would be a royal soul to shine forever on a throne
reared by human love."

Already there had for many years been active religious work, both Catholic and Protestant, among the
lepers at Molokai.  Outside of the colony there were
some two hundred Catholics on the Island.  Once in a
while a priest visited the settlement to administer the

sacraments; and a Father Aubert who had made frequent visits, sometimes staying as long as two weeks, heroically offered to live there permanently. But the offer was not accepted because there was at the time no Catholic church in the colony, services being held in a provisional chapel made of grass. In May, 1872, the Catholic lepers had asked for a permanent church, and one made of wood was shipped from Honolulu, and blessed and dedicated.

The Protestants among the lepers, who outnumbered the Catholics, had had a church built for them, but they had no resident clergyman, the services being in charge of a lay preacher. He seems to have had little influence on their religious life and, having himself contracted leprosy on coming to the Island, later died.

During the agitation for improved conditions at Molokai a convention of all the Protestant denominations in the Islands met and passed a resolution urging that every clergyman be instructed to preach on the duty of isolating lepers. It further petitioned the Government to set aside a day for public fasting and repentance, on which "all might ask God to forgive the sins that had brought about the spread of the disease and to turn the hearts of the people to help in saving the nation." This was the extent of the convention's activities, though it had before it at the time one of those great and rare opportunities that sometimes come to religious organizations. What the lepers really needed was not a fast day, nor any public repentance; the need was for some person to come

among them filled with zeal and courage, and by the
force of his personal influence to make the colony a fit
place for human beings to live in.

Then, on May 10, 1873, a group of Catholic
priests gathered at Wailuku to dedicate a new church.
During a conversation the bishop, Mgr. Maigrêt, mentioned his regret that it was impossible to do anything
for the Molokai lepers, adding that though a missionary had at long intervals visited the Island for a few
days there was no assurance that this practice could
be continued. He was heard by a young Belgian
priest who had been in the Islands for only a few years
and who now volunteered impulsively, "I will go to
Molokai and labor for the poor lepers, whose wretched
state of bodily and spiritual misfortune has often made
my heart bleed within me."

It developed, happily, that at that moment a vessel
was lying in the harbor ready to sail for Molokai with
a cargo of fifty lepers; and two hours after making his
offer, Father Damien, without even a change of clothing or personal effects of any sort with him, and without saying good-bye to his friends, was on the boat with
his bishop, bound for the colony. That evening the
ship returned without him; it had left him—without
supplies or extra clothing—to sleep under the trees in
the open. He was to make the name of this leper
colony famous all over the world. Entering it an
obscure priest, he was to leave—when he died a victim
of leprosy himself—a name blazoned among the names
of humanity's saints and heroes.

# CHAPTER IV

## DAMIEN THE BUILDER

FOR many weeks after Father Damien's arrival at Molokai his only cot was to be the bare ground beneath the *puhala* tree. An uncomfortable cot it must have been, for this tree, one of the few that grow in the Molokai settlement, is found only in rocky places. Its tangle of aërial roots is a breeding ground for scorpions, ants and mosquitoes, and under its widespreading branches fleas and other insects seek shelter from the wind and the rain. At best it is hard to sleep on a rocky surface, and the priest's rest must have been seriously disturbed by the chattering birds and tree rats over his head.

We have no hint as to what his thoughts or plans were that night when the ship had sailed away and darkness had fallen. His proposal to come to the leper settlement was one of the sudden impulses that were so typical of his restless nature. He was never given to considering the cost or the danger of any undertaking. Brother Joseph, who came nearer to him than anyone else during the last years of his life, describes these characteristics thus:

"I picture him as always ready to take up with great vigor anything that presented itself as his actual duty,

60

and, further, anything at all that he thought would be good, whether it was actually his duty or not. Anything that appeared to him to be good—good to do— was something for immediate action; he apparently considered it really his duty. He did not give much time to the study of expediency, or the cost, or the danger."

It is doubtful whether before he went to the dedication of the Wailuku church it had ever occurred to him to go to the leper colony. In the letters written to his brother in Belgium before he went to Molokai we find only one slight reference to leprosy. He writes: "Leprosy is very prevalent here. There are many men covered with it. It does not cause death at once, but it is rarely cured. The disease is dangerous because it is highly contagious." Evidently he had often seen the ravages wrought by the plague. Joseph Dutton quotes him as saying that he had long before been in contact with it, had visited lepers and had heard their confessions in their cabins. His charity, his easily aroused emotions, must have been touched by their sufferings. But he had charge of a large and growing parish, he enjoyed his work, he was loved by his people; and it is not to be believed that before that day at Wailuku he ever intended to offer himself as a missionary to the lepers.

The point is worth emphasis because after his death there was an effort on the part of the forces of religious intolerance and jealousy to depreciate publicly the spirit in which Damien had gone to Molokai. Dr.

C. M. Hyde, for instance, of whom we shall hear more
later, wrote that "he was not sent to Molokai, but went
there without orders." So he did; the statement is
literally true. But the sneer behind it proceeded
from bigotry and jealous resentment. Damien was
not "sent" to Molokai, but he did go with the approval
and the good wishes of his bishop. And years later
this same bishop, realizing the horrible conditions in
the colony and the fact that being sent to it implied
banishment for life, when a priest was needed as
Damien's assistant issued a circular letter to his clergy
asking for volunteers; it was quite within his powers
to "send" someone, to order him to go, but the bishop
did not do this. The way to go to Molokai as a missionary was to volunteer—and that was Damien's way.
Is there, pray, any less credit to be given to the man
who volunteers to go into a hell for his fellow-creatures
than to him who has to be "sent"?

Another sneer, from the same source, alleged that
Damien had gone into his life of sacrifice in order to
become a martyr, to gain fame, to win glory in the next
world. This charge is as absurd as the other. Any
priest to whom the idea might occur was free to carry
it out if he wanted to. And as for future reward,
Damien was a good Catholic and it would have been
strange if he had not had the hope that his good deeds
on earth would be rewarded in heaven. And it is to be
remarked that toward the end of his life he was none
too confident of this requital, for he spent anxious
hours during the final stages of his illness asking him-

self whether he was worthy of Paradise.

It was characteristic, too, of his impulsive and un-deliberating nature that permanent residence at Molokai was no part of his original plan that day. He told Joseph Dutton shortly before his death that when first he came to the Island he expected to stay no more than two or three weeks at longest, and then to return to his parish. Moreover, one of the incidents of the bishop's brief visit of a few hours when he left Damien on the Island was the presentation of the lepers' peti-tion to have a resident priest sent to them. The bishop did not consent, being unwilling to condemn any of his clergy to such a life. He mentions this petition in his diary, saying: "They ask me for a priest who can remain with them, but where to find one?" This entry was made within a few hours after Bishop Maigrêt left Damien to return to Honolulu, and it is certain that both of them then expected that the priest would be back in his own parish within a few weeks.

But the bishop's return without Damien led to a general expectation that the latter was to stay on the Island. On May 13, 1873, the editor of *Nuhou* again wrote:

"We have often said that the poor outcast lepers of Molokai, without physician or pastor, afforded an op-portunity for the exercise of a noble Christian heroism, and we are glad to say that the hero has been found. When the *Kilauea* touched at Kalawao last Saturday, Bishop Maigrêt and Father Damien, a Belgian priest, went ashore. The bishop addressed the lepers with comforting words and introduced the good Father, who had volunteered to live with them and for them. Father Damien was left ashore among the lepers without a home or a change of clothing. We care not what this man's theology may be; he is surely a Christian hero."

Three days later another editorial appeared in the same paper:

"We hope His Majesty will remember the good priest who has gone voluntarily to minister unto His Majesty's lepers on Molokai. If this is not 'a faithful minister of the Gospel' we don't think there is one to be found in these Islands."

Thus, within a few days after Damien left, it seems to have been the general belief that he had gone to stay permanently. The idea led to the sending of various gifts to the bishop, as appears in the following item from the *Honolulu Advertiser* of May 24, 1873:

"Last Sunday several gentlemen happened to be conversing on the fact of Father Damien's having volunteered to live among the lepers of Molokai, when one suggested that they make up a purse for the benefit of the Father. This was done on the spot, and the amount, $130, was given to the bishop to be sent to Damien."

There is no evidence—not even the slightest suggestion—that Damien knew at the time what was being thought and written about him. Yet within a few days

FATHER DAMIEN'S OLD ALTAR, WHICH IS PRESERVED IN THE
PRESENT CHURCH

after arriving at the colony he wrote to the bishop asking to be allowed to stay on, and the bishop acquiesced. This point, too, is emphasized, because of another accusation that was made after Damien's death, the criticism this time being reversed: that he deserved no credit for going, because he did so under his bishop's orders. This charge, revived in 1905 and still cropping up every few years, not only is untrue; it ignores the fact that when he first went there was no suggestion that he was to stay permanently. He may have had this idea in his mind—we cannot tell; but certainly it was never expressed. Probably the determination crystallized during his first few days there as he had borne in on him the desperate needs of the lepers.

It was as a Catholic priest that Damien entered Molokai, to prepare the Catholic lepers for their religious duties. But he soon discovered that he must be far more than priest. He was physician, teacher of the children, carpenter, house-builder, and painter; he was undertaker, digging the graves and making the coffins of those over whom he later read the burial service. Instead of having the spiritual care of two hundred persons in his charge, he found that what was to devolve on him was both the spiritual and the physical care of eight hundred—all the lepers in the colony, Catholic and non-Catholic alike.

His first morning was devoted to taking a census of the eight hundred, of whom he found eighty percent desperately ill, many of them at the point of death. Their crying needs must have been instantly obvious even to a newcomer, and these Damien set about, vigorously and single-handed, meeting as best he might. The conditions he found are described in his report to the Board of Health in 1886:

"In the year 1874 the great question was how to improve the condition of the lepers and their homes. The government appropriation at that time was barely enough to provide them with food. Nearly all the lepers were prostrated on their beds, in damp grass huts, their constitutions badly broken down. The smell of their filth, mixed with the exhalation of their sores, was simply disgusting—unbearable for a newcomer. Many times in fulfilling my priestly duties in their huts I have had to close my nostrils and run outside for fresh air. To counteract the bad smell I accustomed myself to using a pipe, whose smoke helped somewhat to prevent my carrying in my clothing the obnoxious odor of the lepers. At that time the progress of the disease was fearful, the rate of mortality high."

A later passage describes his effort to get better and more substantial dwellings for his charges:

"A heavy windstorm blew down most of the rotten abodes, and many a weaker leper lay in the wind and rain with his blanket and clothing wet. In a few days the grass under the sleeping-mats began to give forth an unpleasant odor. I called the attention of the agent to the fact at once and demanded lumber. The authorities, aided by the gifts of friends, sent a schooner loaded with scantling with which to build solid frames. All lepers in distress received the material needed for the erection of these frames, with inch-square laths to thatch the grass or the sugarcane leaves to. Afterward we procured rough boards, and from private and charitable sources shingles and flooring. Those who had a little money hired carpenters; for those without means, the priest with his own leper boys did the work of erecting a good many small houses. Thus the dwellings improved."

This boatload of lumber sent by the Government was the direct result of Damien's demand that the agent send a request to the Board of Health; and the laths and boards contributed by charitable donors were the fruit of the begging that he did during his first visit back to Honolulu, a few weeks after he went to the colony.

It was during these early weeks that he first came into conflict with the Board of Health, a conflict that was to continue till his death. Brother Dutton explains the situation by describing certain traits in Damien, whom he speaks of as

"vehement and excitable in regard to matters that did not seem to him right, and [he] sometimes said and did things which he afterward regretted. I am safe in saying that, in all the differences, he had a true desire to do right, to bring about what he thought was best. No doubt he erred sometimes in judgment, as all of us do. These things make his relations with the Government officials more readily understood. With some they were better than with others; with all better at some times than at other times.   In certain periods he got along smoothly with everyone, and at all times he was urgent for improvements, or what he thought were such.   The carrying out of things done by the Government was facilitated by his actions.   In some cases he made for confusion, as the various authorities would not agree with him.   I believe that his efforts for the people here for material improvement have been beneficial to the place.   In spiritual matters he did great good."

This frank analysis by the man who was closest to Damien gives perhaps the truest key to his character. We must remember that he was an energetic, impulsive priest from the Belgian peasant class.   It casts no discredit on his memory to admit that the time when he volunteered to take his brother's place as a missionary in the South Seas was a time when the Church did not insist that its missionaries have the long technical schooling that is required today.   Because of the scarcity of priests and the pressing needs of the missions, the Society of the Sacred Hearts of Jesus and Mary, which had charge of the mission to the Sandwich Islands (as they were called then), did not in Damien's day require the one-year novitiate, the two years of philosophy, and the four years of theology obligatory now.   Indeed, Damien did not have even the training of the average priest of his own time.   No doubt he was a poor theologian—and considering what he had to do, it is probably just as well that he was; no Louvain scholar would have been contented at Molokai. But he was zealous, and the slow caution of the Board's procedure must have been both incomprehensible and exasperating to him. Before his eyes daily were hundreds of wretched men and women whose stay in this world was brief at best and whose sufferings meantime cried to be relieved; and the sight roused his impatience of official deliberateness. To him the needs of the lepers he loved had first claim on the attention of the authorities. We can understand why in their eyes he was "obstinate, headstrong, brusque, and officious." He certainly was all these; and no doubt, in order to win what he considered essential for his lepers, he had to be.

After he had been for some weeks on the Island he returned to Honolulu to perform certain religious duties, to procure supplies, to interest wealthy persons in the lepers' needs if possible, and to lay his plans before the bishop. His quest was successful; he obtained an entire shipload of clothes and food, and another ship—the one carrying the lumber—was soon to sail. Here, too, he had his first real clash with the authorities.

On the point of sailing, he remembered that he had not called on the president of the Board of Health, whom he wished to acquaint with his plans and hopes. This official received him coldly and ordered him to return at once to Molokai, warning him never again to visit the larger Island. Further, Damien was told that if ever he crossed the mountains separating the colony from the rest of Molokai he would be arrested

and imprisoned.  Vainly he pleaded that there would
be occasions when he must come to Honolulu to see
his bishop.  He was told that once he returned to
Molokai he could never leave it again.  And within
a few days after his return to the colony he got an
official notice to the effect that if he ever tried to leave,
or to visit any other part of the Island, he would be
put under arrest.  At once he replied, in a short but
firm letter, that he would leave the Island whenever
he wanted to do so.

In this connection there is interest in an episode
that happened a few weeks afterward.  A priest who
wanted to visit Damien took passage on a vessel that
was to carry another group of lepers to the colony.
When the ship anchored off Kalaupapa the captain
told the priest that, by order of the authorities, he
could not land.  Meanwhile Damien—who made a
practice of holding mass at four o'clock in the morning
on days when the boat came in, so as to be at the water-
front to greet newcomers—had heard about his visitor.
Learning that the latter was not to be allowed to land,
Damien got a canoe and paddled out to the ship.
When he was about to board it, the captain told him
to keep away, since he must not communicate with
anyone.  Then Damien, standing up in the canoe,
asked his superior (who was at the rail) to hear his
confession.  And there, in the hearing of passengers
and crew, he made his confession and received the
sacramental absolution.

These regulations continued in force for about six

months. During that period, though he did not go to Honolulu, there were times when he climbed the narrow, winding path that threaded the cliffs behind the settlement, and visited other parts of the Island. Then a new king came to the throne, pressure was exerted from various quarters, and the police order was rescinded: henceforth he might visit Honolulu as often as he wanted. He took advantage of the permission several times during his residence at Molokai, and often was entertained in the royal palace itself.

In a letter dated November 25, 1873, to his brother (who later was himself to be a priest at the colony), Damien describes his first few months among the lepers.

"God has deigned to choose your unworthy brother to help the poor people attacked by that horrible malady, leprosy. Shut off in a corner of Molokai, between inaccessible cliffs and the sea, these unfortunate creatures are condemned to perpetual banishment. Out of two thousand who have been sent here some eight hundred are living, among them a certain number of Catholics. A priest was wanted; but here was a difficulty . . . A priest placed here must consider himself shut up with lepers for the rest of his life. Remembering that on the day of my profession I had put myself under the funeral pall, I offered myself . . . to meet . . . this second death.

"Let me give a picture of my work. Imagine a collection of huts, with eight hundred lepers. No doctor; and since there is no cure there seems to be no place for a doctor. A white man who is a leper, and your humble servant, do all the doctoring. Sometimes I do feel repugnance when I have to hear the confessions of those who, near their end, have wounds filled with maggots. Often I hardly know how to administer extreme unction when both the hands and the feet are nothing but raw sores. I have just built a chapel two miles from here, and did most of the carpenter work myself."

The tone of this letter shows clearly that by the time of writing it—six months after his arrival—he had become fixed in his intention to stay. By this time, too, he had made a start on certain tasks that had at once presented themselves as needing to be undertaken without delay. The first of these was the improvement of the inadequate water-supply. Not only was it insufficient, but the distance that the water must be carried—from springs at the base of the cliffs—meant that many of the people often had none at all. Damien said that when he arrived they were carrying water to their huts in oilcans. Sometimes it was so scarce that, save for a small spring near the huts, there was barely enough to drink. He began at once to pester the Government agent, until his continual complaints forced the man to make a report to the higher authorities. The result was that a pipe was run down from the springs to the settlement, with taps placed at intervals. Though the pipe was small, and there were no spare fittings or extra couplings with which to repair the frequent breaks, yet the new system was far better than the old. Further relief was obtained when a small reservoir was built.

This matter attended to, he set about to remedy a second crying evil. The lepers had been herded together in tiny grass huts through which the rain swept and which every wind blew down. To such dwellings as these the word "house" could hardly be applied, all being of a makeshift character owing to the scarcity of building material. Many families had no huts of their own, and these small, crude shelters were therefore crowded with men and women huddled together indiscriminately. The consequent sanitary conditions, the lack of ventilation, cannot be described. And in every hut lay some man or woman at the point of death.

These conditions Damien set forth in vigorous complaints to the agent, with the result that the materials mentioned were sent from Honolulu and he could start building. No fewer than three hundred cottages were put up, most of the work being done by his own hands with the aid of the leper boys of his church. They were very simple dwellings, even crude, but being set on trestles raised from the ground they were considerably better than the former flimsy grass huts. The ultimate consequence of the beginning he made toward improved housing for his lepers is that today the Molokai villages are filled with white wooden cottages, even more comfortable than many of those inhabited by healthy Hawaiians on the other Islands.

To the day of his death the food supply for the col-

ony was to be the subject of a never-ending battle between Damien and the Board of Health.   Though it
had long ago become obvious that the lepers could not
be expected to raise their own, it took the authorities
years to realize either what amount must be provided
or what kind; because the kind of food a leper eats
plays an important part in the progress of his disease.
No real improvement in either direction was made
until Damien's sharp demands forced it.   Even five
years after he came, he had to tell a visiting committee
who asked what they ought to do toward better conditions, "Provide more food!"

Again, eighteen years after the settlement was
founded—in 1884—the Princess Regent of the Islands,
with her daughter, made a visit to the colony.   They
were shocked by what they saw there.   The Queen
spoke to the lepers, whereupon some of them were allowed to express their views of what should be done
for them.   The first speaker said: "Chief among the
ills of which we complain are poor and insufficient
food and the lack of proper nursing; if the Government cannot supply these it should send us home.
Our clothing allowance of six dollars will buy only a
shirt and a blanket.   And we need better water."
The second speaker, too, spoke of the food and clothing and of the lack of water and medical attention.
The under-superintendent of the settlement, Mr.
Hutchinson, himself a leper, agreed with the other
complainants and emphasized the need of medical
equipment, though he was the Board of Health's em-

ployee. Indeed, during the whole visit of the Princess she heard nothing but complaints; but after her visit there was some improvement in the food supply.

But we find Damien continuing his efforts two years later. In a report written in 1888 he said that of the lepers outside the hospital not one-tenth had tasted milk for several years. And as long as he lived he hammered at this point of more and better food for the colony; one of his last letters shows that as he reached the end of his life he wanted his people given not their bare necessaries only but also a few simple luxuries. And always, along with his fight for food, went an effort to get the six-dollar clothing allowance increased.

We have mentioned Damien's practical services in replacing the frail grass huts of the people with stronger structures. At first he cut down trees with his own hands, in order to put together some more adequate shelters for the worst cases. Carpentry was one of his hobbies, and when he felt that enough houses had been built he spent some of his spare time in making window-frames, doors, and bathtubs, which were given to any who could use them. For several years he made nearly all the coffins; it is said that during his life on the Island he made altogether nearly a thousand of these.

He was not only carpenter; he was doctor as well. When there was no resident physician he issued drugs from the supply kept in his own hut and himself treated the sick. As late as 1887 he was still bathing the helpless patients, dressing sores, and doing anything of this kind that came to his hand. It may be noted that during his life on Molokai he buried more than 1600 lepers.

Much of his time had to be spent in caring for the sick. For many years after he came the hospital continued in charge of the non-medical man already mentioned, with volunteer untrained nurses, and Damien helping. Besides supplying medicines and washing and dressing the patients he assisted in simple operations. Yet no medical attention, however skilled and thorough, could have effected more than a slight alleviation of the disease, since in that day no cure was known; indeed, when a patient was sent to the hospital it was customary to send a coffin with him in the same cart.

Another pressing problem was the morals of the colony. Damien found on his arrival that the place had its gamblers and card-sharps, its women of easy virtue, its illicit distillers, and various other criminals who had demoralized the entire colony. With these he was to wage a long battle in which no quarter was given, and in which he was sometimes forced to appeal to the authorities for help. But in the end he overcame them. It is evident now that many of the vicious and lying stories that were later circulated about him emanated from the men and women whose influence he had combated.

In the report of 1886 he describes the moral conditions he found when he came:

"Before my arrival . . . it was said that as a rule vice reigned instead of virtue. When new lepers came, the old ones were eager to impress them with the principle: *aole kanawai ma keia wahi*—'In this place there is no law.' I was obliged to fight against such defiance of Divine as well as human laws. The consequence of this impious principle was that the people—mostly unmarried—were living promiscuously without distinction of sex, and many an unfortunate woman had had to become a prostitute in order to win friends who might care for her and her children. When she was attacked by the disease, she and her children were cast out and had to find another shelter; sometimes they were thrust behind a stone wall and left there to die, or they were carried to the hospital and deserted.

"Another source of immorality was intemperance. There grows along the side of the mountains a plant that the natives call *ki,* whose root when fermented and distilled yields a highly intoxicating liquor which, owing to the crude and imperfect distilling process, is unfit for drinking. The distilling of this liquor was being carried on to a horrible extent when I arrived, and its consequences can be more easily imagined than described on paper. Under its influence the natives would abandon all decency and run about naked and acting as though mad. The authorities had tried to stop the distilling but had been unsuccessful. The agent and I went around, and at last, by threats and persuasion, got the natives to give up their stills; some of the guiltiest were convicted, and then pardoned on condition that they never resume the practice. But for a long time, under the influence of the liquor they neglected everything except prostitution and drinking."

In Damien's eyes his most important duty, however, was the spiritual care of the people.   He was a priest, and an earnest, faithful priest, untiring in his work on behalf of the mission under his charge and always busy devising means for extending its influence and increasing its membership.   He had found awaiting him a small chapel, at Kalawao in the shade of the cliffs, and at once he set to work to build another at Kalaupapa, where the boats landed.   This church was built largely by his own hands, with the help of such members of his flock as could work.   Later, too, he built a church to replace the small Kalawao chapel and at the same time started an orphanage.

When Damien came to the settlement its non-Catholics outnumbered those of his faith, and at first the chapel attendance was slim and his funds scanty.   But he made an intensive drive for membership and money, and by the time of his death two-thirds of the lepers were Catholics and in buildings and funds his congregation had twice the property of the Protestant groups.   If Damien, on looking over his congregation on Sunday, missed any of his flock, on Monday bright and early he would be at their huts, asking where they had been at church time.   Only illness was accepted as an excuse.

As his parish grew he established a system by which his members, under his direction, built their own homes out of funds that had been bequeathed to the church. The effect of this was that many of the Catholics' houses were larger and far more substantial than those provided by the Government. As a rule the Catholic lepers willed their houses to the parish. Since these mission houses were not overcrowded, new arrivals—especially if they had families—were always eager to secure one of them; and doubtless many became converts with this end in view. But if afterward they failed to live up to what Damien considered their religious responsibilities he would warn them, several times, and then if they continued lax he evicted them and sent them to one of the Government houses.

Nor was his work confined to the promontory on which the colony was located. For some years the entire Island was his parish. Climbing the narrow trail that wound over the cliffs he visited distant parts of Molokai, organized congregations whose chapels he built with his own hands, and helped the priests in various parts of the Island. Always he was driven by zeal for the faith he served, a zeal that reached all to whom he considered that his duty extended. It was this unremitting ardor, doubtless, that led Dr. Hyde later to call him "bigoted and intolerant." Hyde may have meant by this that Damien took his religious beliefs seriously and tried to win converts to the faith he served. But if he was implying the charge that Damien ever refused help to non-Catholics, it was an utterly false accusation. In the beginning Damien's help was given without distinction to Catholics, Protestants, and natives who clung to their own religion. Later on, when the authorities assumed better control over the settlement, Damien's work gradually limited itself more and more to those of his own faith. But to call him bigoted merely because he was a devoted and energetic Catholic missionary is absurd.

Another of Hyde's allegations was to the effect that Damien "had no hand in the reforms and improvements inaugurated, which were the work of our Board of Health, as occasion required and means were provided. . . . Others have done much for the lepers— our own ministers, the Government physicians, and so forth." This again is utterly untrue, and Hyde knew better than to make such a charge. The reforms did not come about until after Damien had been at the settlement for many years. It was long after his arrival before a resident doctor was appointed or enough medical supplies were provided. It was not from the Board of Health that the pressure came for more food and clothing for the Molokai lepers. Years afterward, the Board did take over the temporal and physical care of the colony, and its activities under the United States Government made of Molokai the most efficient leper settlement in the world. But in the old days it was Father Damien, and he alone, who by his force of character, his determination to bring about better conditions, his dogged efforts to rouse slumbering officialdom to a sense of its duty—Father Damien it was who (to adopt an expression that would hardly have been understood in his day) "put Molokai on the map."

One dream obsessed the man, an ambition that he could not resist talking about with other Catholics on every occasion: the idea that the leper settlement might some day be developed into a special and highly organized diocese of his Church. Even though it might not be fulfilled for many years, still he thought of himself, perhaps, as a sort of apostolic vicar to the lepers, with special powers and privileges conferred on him by the Pope. He pictured the work of the settlement as controlled by strict ecclesiastical rules somewhat like those we saw operating in the medieval monasteries. He may indeed have known about these institutions and their work among the lepers, and have dreamed that such a work might again come into being.

But this was only a dream. The present reality was hard and unremitting work, work that had to be done alone, that forced him to rush from one task to another, seeing everything to be done at once, having to start a fresh undertaking before being able to finish the one already started, never pausing, never resting. It was a herculean task for one man with practically no help. At one time he acted as assistant superintendent of the colony, but the experiment was not a success: he had trouble with his superior, there was rebellion against his authority, and in time the Board of Health appointed another person to the position.

Several priests at one time or another came to the settlement for short periods. Father Andrew Burgerman arrived in 1874, but his duty was the care of the

Catholics outside the colony. He lived at the colony for four months while Damien built a chapel for him on the other side of the mountains. Father Andrew paid a few visits to the settlement afterward, and in 1878 moved there, to live in the village of Kalaupapa until 1880. But of this priest Damien complained again and again that he was too independent, and not even-tempered; the two did not get along very well together. Apparently it was a case of friction between two temperaments that were too much alike.

This inability of Damien's to agree always with his co-workers is further illustrated by the case of Father Albert Montiton, the next priest to come. Montiton arrived in the latter part of 1882 and remained almost three years. Once more Damien could not get along with his fellow-worker, and the two continued to clash. When Damien complained to his bishop of being left alone to carry on the work, the bishop commented thus: "Father Albert would still be with him if he [Damien] were a little more accommodating with his fellow-priests, and less of an autocrat."

But in 1886 there came to Molokai a lay worker who was to become Father Damien's firm friend and whose name was in after years to become known throughout the world—Ira Dutton, better known as Brother Joseph. This American came to the island on July 29, 1886. He was for years Damien's closest associate, and carried on the work after Damien's death.

Assistance in his responsibility for the leper orphans came in November, 1888, a few months before his death, when three Franciscan Sisters whose mother house was in Syracuse, New York, came to take charge of the orphan girls. Five years before, a group of Sisters from this Order had come to the Hawaiian Islands, and now the Mother Superior had sent three of them to the branch hospital at Molokai. They did a valuable work, though their own special duties were such that they could give Damien little direct help. By this time his mission had grown powerful and there were enough workers for its needs. An orphanage for boys had been opened, and some schools. But it was not until a few months before Damien's death that any priest came who was to stay long.

For years Damien had been in correspondence with a fellow-countryman, Father Lambert Conrardy. Father Conrardy seems to have written the first letter, from a missionary parish among the Indians of Oregon. He had heard of the Molokai work and wanted to share it. The proposal appealed to Damien and he set to work to have it executed. But the bishop preferred to have Conrardy take a novitiate in Europe before coming to Molokai; there had been some trouble in the Islands with wandering priests, and the bishop did not want any more. Damien protested rather heatedly, saying that such training was unnecessary and demanding that the man be allowed to come at once. In the end the bishop gave in, and Father Conrardy arrived in 1888.

The bishop's concession stirred up some resentment among the other priests in his diocese. They felt that

his action in letting a man come in from the outside
would create the impression that they themselves were
unwilling to work at Molokai, that they were not willing to face isolation and possible infection.    The
bishop thereupon wrote a circular letter to his clergy
in order to allay any such suspicion.    In it he asked
for volunteers who would go to the colony.    Only one
of the priests failed to reply, all the others declaring
themselves ready to go whenever their superior wished.
The appointment went to Father Wendelin Moellers,
a cool-headed, even-tempered man, and he arrived at
the settlement only seven months before Damien died.

For now Damien was facing death.    How long the
disease had been lurking in his system there is no way
of knowing.    But one Sunday morning the lepers were
to hear their priest address them in a new way.    He
had always before begun his sermon with the word
*Brethren*.    But on this day what they heard when he
began to speak to them was *We lepers*. . . .

# CHAPTER V

## GREATER LOVE THAN THIS

How we shall decide the date on which Father Damien first realized that he had been stricken with leprosy depends on which of two stories we accept. His brother, Father Pamphile, in the short collection of Damien letters that he published, says that the earliest suspicion arose in 1884, but that it was not until 1885 that suspicion became certainty. But Father Pamphile does not mention how he got his information. One day, he says, his brother, having been tramping the dusty roads of the colony, decided to take a hot foot-bath. He plunged his feet into the steaming tub and felt no sensation of heat. The water was scalding hot, and its effects on his skin could be seen, but feeling there was none. He knew what this meant, for one of the first symptoms of leprosy is the insensitiveness of the affected part. He had always realized, from the day of his coming, that this moment might some time arrive; and now the plague had set its mark on him. Ahead of him now lay death—certain and horrible death.

Yet there is another story, told by Brother Joseph Dutton in a letter. This account was given to Brother Joseph by Damien himself five weeks before his death on April 15, 1889; because of the close intimacy of the two men, it is worth attention. The priest told Brother Joseph that one morning when he was shaving he overturned the cup of scalding water on his bare foot; he felt no sensation, and thus realized that he was a leper. This, too, is placed in 1885.

Which story we believe, however, is of little consequence, because there is evidence that he was infected long before he himself realized it; others knew it. Dr. Mouritz, for instance, who took up his work as physician to the settlement in 1884, has described his first sight of Damien. The priest was then forty-four years old, active and vigorous, weighing about 244 pounds. The doctor says that his profile was that of a handsome man (something no one else ever said), and then goes on to speak of the color of his skin—a dark copper color. "It was visible proof," he adds, "of the invasion of the destroyer."

In any case, we know that from 1885 onward the progress of the disease was so rapid that we can only conclude that he must already have been suffering from it for years. He must have had some suspicion of this at an earlier date. Toward the end of 1884 he grew somewhat worried over his health and consulted a Dr. Arning who had come to Molokai to study leprosy. Although it was to be six months before any clear external signs appeared, Arning decided that his patient had leprosy. Diagnosis was difficult, but there seemed to be some destruction of the nerves of the knee.

The strongest confirmation of the probability that Damien had the disease before 1885 is found in Brother Joseph's notes of his conversations with the priest. Covering three sheets of paper these constitute a record of Damien's last illness as told to his friend during the final weeks, and they go into much detail about his physical condition over a period of some years. These notes, found along with other material about the colony, were sent by Brother Joseph after Damien's death to Bishop Hermann, then Catholic bishop of the Islands. The rest of the manuscript is a commentary written by Dutton after Damien's death and is cast in the form of a legal affidavit. The notes give us the following information:

"Rev. Father J. Damien De Veuster, Catholic priest, native of Belgium; Belgian parents; 49 years of age. All members of family strong, no taint of syphilis. No relatives on Islands. Served as priest on the Island of Hawaii from 1864 until 1873. . . . Heard confession of lepers; ministered to them sometimes in their cabins, but had no constant nor very particular contact with them until [he] came here to leper settlement; from which time until now, contact and association almost constant. In 1873 was strong and healthy with remarkably robust constitution. . . . Is quite sure that when near to lepers, as at confession or in their cabins—before coming to the leper settlement—felt on each occasion a peculiar sensation in the face, a sort of burning or itching, and that [he] felt the same here at the settlement during the first two or three years; that

he also felt it on the legs. Is confident that the germs
were in system within first three years of residence
here; can trace it back positively to 1876. Small dry
spots appeared at that time, particularly on arms; some
on the back. On these spots perspiration did not appear as elsewhere. Upon treatment . . . would disappear, but return again. In 1877 and '78 [they]
assumed yellowish color and became larger. This
describes the first marks. But earlier still feet had a
peculiar sensation; were hot and feverish. . . . Could
not sleep without first giving them a cold-water soak;
nor, without doing this, keep them covered at night.
This was in 1874 and '75."

The dates in this statement include the year after
Damien came to Molokai; after his death it was said—
and is believed even today by some persons in Hawaii
—that he had contracted leprosy before starting for the
settlement, and that the story of his volunteering to go
was issued in an attempt to hide the fact that the authorities had decided to segregate him with the other
outcasts. Those who repeated this version of the affair
explained that the officials did not want to force a
priest openly to accept segregation and so allowed him
to make the gesture of volunteering. But no evidence
has ever been adduced to support this version; on the
contrary, the Government had nothing to do with
Damien's going to Molokai.

However, the passage above that tells of the sensa-
tions in face and legs early in his residence at Molokai

FATHER DAMIEN TWO MONTHS BEFORE HIS DEATH

suggests the probability that the disease was already
on him when he came, contracted not at the settlement
but in some hut on Hawaii after he arrived at the
Islands in March, 1864. We note that, though he told
Dutton that it was the overturning of the shaving
water that made him realize he was a leper, this episode is not mentioned in the notes taken from his reminiscences before his death. It doubtless happened, but
it did not actually mark the beginning of his realization. There is more evidence on this point in the
notes, which we quote further:

"In 1881 began to be badly troubled with severe
pains in the feet, especially in the left one; and in
1882 sciatic nerve trouble came on, clearly defined,
all along the left leg. At the close of 1882, or early in
1883, entire insensibility of one side of left foot took
place, and so remains to this day. . . . Able to draw
a line marking division of the sensitive from the in-
sensitive portion of the foot. This is the only part of
the body so attacked. The pain of sciatic nerve and
of the inside (big toe side) of the foot was intense and
almost constant, accompanied by formation of nodes
in the left groin. All of these pains disappeared at
once, about June, 1885. Then the right ear became
swollen, with tubercular enlargement making the
whole thing an immense affair. At the same time began the disfigurement of person in a general and
marked manner. . . . The foot that was partly in-
sensible was for a long time exceedingly weak. Now,

since the disease has spread over the body, it becomes strong again.

Correct

(*Signed*) J. Damien De Veuster

*priest"*

March 10, 1889

From these notes it seems possible to trace the course of Damien's leprosy. Assuming that he already carried its germs in 1873, we find him first noticing symptoms within three years afterward; speaking of 1877 he uses the phrase "first marks." Evidently, long before the doctors pronounced him a leper the signs of the disease were visible. He appears in the beginning to have had the anæsthetic form, which attacks the nervous system. In the last three years it was the tubercular form, whose progress is rapid and easily seen. His eyebrows fell out, both ears were enlarged, and face and hands became greatly swollen. Sores broke out on hands and wrists; his nose was obstructed and the bridge fell in; at times he had great difficulty in breathing. He found it almost impossible to use his hands because of the hard, enlarged lumps that took the place of knuckles. From the time that the disease was clearly leprosy its progress was rapid.

That he should have become infected is only natural. He seems not to have feared the contagion, nor to have worried over the danger of contracting it; but he used caution at first. We saw how he preferred sleeping in the open to sharing a leper's hut; and six months after his arrival he wrote to his brother that he was living in a hut that he himself had built, cooking his own meals, doing his own washing, and not allowing any leper to enter the place. Perhaps if he had persisted in such precautions, if he had taken even ordinary care to ward off infection, he might have escaped the plague entirely. Yet this persistent care may have been impracticable in combination with the work he had set out to do; or he may simply have abandoned—more or less unconsciously—his early attitude of watchfulness; or finally, it is possible that he decided that he could hardly hope to escape permanently, however cautious he might be. One thing is certain: that he lived out his days side by side with the people he loved, always cheerful and apparently care-free, taking no precautions after the first few months. Once he was asked whether he was not afraid of contracting the disease, and he smiled as he replied: "If Providence sees fit to afflict me while I am working among lepers, whether I am worthy or not I shall gain a Crown of Thorns." There seems to have been a certain sort of cheerful fatalism beneath his attitude.

Many details are preserved that demonstrate how careless he eventually became. He kept the lepers out of his house only a few months; soon it was open to the whole settlement. A leper cooked the priest's food, handling both the food and the dishes with hands that were covered with open sores. His clothes were washed by a leper woman. Day and night his house was open, and lepers came to eat at his table and sleep on his bed. He would lay down his pipe; a leper would pick it up; and Damien would then resume

smoking it.   While he was building the houses he used
the same tools that his leper boys had handled with
their sore hands.   In the huts he followed the natives'
customs; when for instance the pipe was passed around
he took his turn.   He brought food and drink to the
dying, washed their sores, swept their huts.   If he
chanced to visit a hut at meal-time he ate *poi* after
the native manner, dipping his hands into the dish
that had already been dipped into by the sore hands
of the lepers.   Again and again he was warned against
all these things by the medical men; they even told
him that he was setting a bad example for the non-
lepers of the colony.   But no advice, no warning, could
make him cautious.   He seems to have been absolutely
without fear.

The same carelessness characterized his choice of a
site for his house.   It stood close to the lepers' burial
ground, containing more than a thousand bodies.
Since the ground was rocky it was impossible to dig
the graves deep; coffins were piled on one another, and
bodies were often buried without coffins.   The graves
were disturbed by wild pigs and by the scavenger dogs
that were a pest in the settlement.   The air was thick
with flies and other insects.   Dr. Mouritz reported that
the conditions were indescribable, and likened the
pervading odor to that of a charnel house.   Damien
was insistent on plenty of fresh air and sanitary precautions for his people; for himself he was not so particular.   Yet we should perhaps not be too hasty in
criticizing him, since any more careful mode of life

may well have been out of the question if he was to
live among his people and help them daily and hourly.

In the latter part of 1885, when the progress of his
disease grew markedly more rapid and its signs were
plain to be seen on his features, a new treatment for
leprosy began to be talked about—the Gotō treatment
used in Japan.  Of course, various "cures" were always
being advertised, and, because medical science had so
little hope of combating leprosy effectively, sufferers
were quick to seize at any prospect of relief.  This
Gotō treatment, however, was not represented as a
cure but was merely a method used for some years in
Japan that had relieved certain of the more hideous
phenomena of the disease.  So to Honolulu Damien
went to enter the hospital and undergo this treatment
for several weeks.  It was a combination of hot baths
and drugs and, because its details were kept secret
from the medical profession at large, it was a very ex-
pensive affair.  But Damien was a restless patient,
longing to get back to his work; and he returned to
Molokai after two weeks.

By this time it was generally known among those
who were interested that Damien was a leper.  He had
told the bishop of his fate in the letter that had led the
bishop to urge him to come to Honolulu for the Gotō
treatment, as we have seen that he did, in spite of the
opening protest: "I cannot come to Honolulu, for
leprosy has attacked me.  There are signs of it on my
left cheek and ear, and my eyebrows are beginning to
fall.  I shall soon be quite disfigured.  As I have no

doubt of the real character of the malady I remain calm, resigned, and very happy in the midst of my people."

We may quote, too, from a letter written to his family toward the end of 1885. Although sent to his brother it was, like all his infrequent letters home, addressed to "my dear mother, brothers, and all the members of the family." He spoke here of his life at Molokai, saying that every Sunday he celebrated mass twice, preached four times, and held benediction twice. "In the evening I am usually very tired," he wrote, adding that since March he had been the only priest at the settlement. Mentioning that his mother was "now of a venerable age," he hoped that she was in good health. But though he had known of his leprosy for some months he did not speak of it, not wishing to pain her.

But the fact could not be kept secret. His Honolulu visit told the world that what everyone had long expected had at last happened. The news was carried to every quarter of the globe, and expressions of sympathy began to pour in. Until this time Damien had been a lonely figure, known only to his Church. Now the whole world claimed him as one of its heroic souls. And it was not Catholics alone who hailed this noble martyrdom; even warmer was the praise of the Protestant world. This was perhaps only natural, since courageous and self-sacrificing devotion had been familiar in the annals of the Catholic Church for centuries past. But to the world in general the picture of

Father Damien seemed almost unique in the annals
of the ages, and apparently it could not be too often
retold.   Gifts began to pour in on Molokai, alms and
donations from all parts of the earth.   England was
particularly generous.   The Rev. Hugh Chapman,
rector of St. Luke's Church (Anglican) in Camberwell,
London, at once started a fund for Damien's mission.
Before Damien's death more than $10,000 had been
contributed from various sources.   Another English-
man, Edward Clifford, moved by the accounts he read
in the English press, set out for Molokai to visit the
dying priest, and the announcement of his intention
brought a flood of requests for him to take gifts and
money with him.   Every mail brought to Molokai
suggested cures for leprosy from all over the world;
though these were in general odd and useless, Damien
did try some of them.   Now he was no longer alone—
all humanity, it seemed, had turned its eyes to the
leper colony.

It was through a Belgian newspaper story that the
tidings came first to his family.   It was sensationally
written, its details heightened and exaggerated for the
sake of effect: Damien's flesh was falling off in rags—
his hands and feet had dropped off—and so forth.
Some officious person with too little judgment read
this account to Damien's mother, who was ill at the
time—indeed was to die shortly afterward.   At its end
she only said, "Well, then, we shall go to heaven together!"   And after her death a letter from Molokai
told the family that the newspaper story had been true

in only one of its many horrible details.

This letter, to Pamphile, was written by Damien himself, and at a date when his mother was still alive. He speaks of his love and constant thought for her, and goes on to talk of his own illness; casually, as though it were of no great importance and also as if they already knew about it. "My malady seems to be yielding somewhat to the Japanese treatment that I have been undergoing for five weeks." He was very busy, he told them, because the work of building the large Government hospital was under his personal direction; he was thus unable to write them at any great length.

He had gone on with the Gotō treatment for some time after returning from Honolulu, having established the system of baths at Kalawao. Being Damien, he overdid both the baths and the medicine, however, sitting for long periods in water at a temperature of 108° F.; and instead of being helped he was rather harmed by this excess. Dr. Mouritz, who saw him at this time, says that after a course of these baths Damien tottered when he walked, and his clothes hung on him like bags. Yet, in spite of all the evidence that for him at least this treatment was unsuitable, he persisted in saying for a time that it was doing him good. In the end he had to admit, however, that the hot baths were actually undermining his constitution.

Though he was now growing rapidly worse, he continued as active as he had ever been, if not indeed more so. Ill he might be, with death only a few

THE OFFICE AND COTTAGE OF THE MANAGER

months off; but there was work to be done, and he was the man to do it. Sunday after Sunday he said mass; Sunday after Sunday he struggled into the pulpit to preach to his people, of whom he was now one in very truth. Through the week there were the new hospital and the new church to be built for which he must act as both architect and carpenter. With his own fate heavy upon him he must still visit the lepers—"the *other* lepers," now—urging them to set their lives in order before they died and tending their physical needs with his own hands as in all the years past. He had never spared himself before; he did not spare himself now.

"Why don't you rest, Father Damien?" he was asked. "Rest!" he retorted. "It's no time to rest now, when there is so much left to do and my time is so short!" And asked whether he did not hope that he might be cured he replied in words that will never be forgotten: "I would not be cured if the price of my cure were that I must leave the Island and give up my work!" Here was no pose, no affectation, but rather the voicing of the one dominant motive of his life, his overmastering passion for the colony to which he had given everything that was in him. Molokai was his world.

That during this last act of his tragedy he was left so largely without helpers is not to be held against his official superiors, for they did make some effort to send him assistance; this had become the more necessary since the increased funds had so enlarged the scope of the colony's activities. During the final eight months he had other priests to help him. But the authorities realized, better than anyone else, how unwilling Damien would be to delegate any of his duties as long as he had strength to get about. "I am going to die in harness," he wrote. Moreover he did not work well with others; he was too much the autocrat. And if he worked on alone, it was because that was the only way he would or could work.

One of his helpers should be mentioned especially, because his story, too, is the story of devotion to an ideal. In November, 1887, there came to Molokai a Father Gregoire Archambeaux, who was to remain with Damien for four months. This French priest was a leper who expected to help in the work of the mission. But besides his leprosy he had asthma, and soon after his arrival he found that he could not stand the damp climate. In March, 1888, he was taken to the hospital at Kakaako, where he died at the end of the year.

Brother Joseph has already entered this story; he will not leave it for nearly fifty years. Quite unheralded this American appeared at the colony on July 29, 1886. In the world he was Ira Dutton; at Molokai, Brother Joseph. During the Civil War he had been an officer in the Union Army. Having been converted to Catholicism and wishing to give himself to a life of service—"to help my neighbors and to fill out a penance which I feel necessary"—he had, on hearing of Damien's work, paid his own way to the Islands and there offered his services as medical dresser. On the

day when these two men met, the impulsive priest and
the calm, serene lay brother, there came together two
souls whose purposes were identical and whose names
were to be linked forever.   Dutton was to become
Damien's closest friend, to work with him, eat with
him, and carry on his work after his death.

By the end of 1887 the marked changes in Damien's
physical condition brought changes equally marked in
his temperament.   His face was now much disfigured,
and every movement increased the difficulty of breathing.   Now, too, instead of being his old eager and
active self, overcheerful at some times and easily irri-
tated at others, he grew calmer and at the same time
strangely gloomy.   This depression, which was an
effect of the disease, lasted only a few months.   He
would sometimes drop his work and fall silent, staring
fixedly ahead at nothing.   Two things were worrying
him.   The first was natural: "Who will look after my
poor orphan boys and girls when I am gone?"   But
this question was presently met satisfactorily by the
assurance that Brother Joseph would undertake the
responsibility.   The other care seems stranger, considering what Damien's life had been: was he worthy
of the heaven that he had so long preached as the reward of the faithful?

But we cannot leave this aspect of his last days without emphasizing again how unlike Damien it was to
be depressed.   The leper colony was not entirely a
melancholy place, and that it was not must be credited
largely to Damien's natural disposition.   The lepers

knew him as a cheerful and light-hearted friend.  He
was always willing to leave off work for a time and
join the children at their play.  On almost any day he
could be seen surrounded by romping, laughing
youngsters, playing tag with them or joining in other
childish games.  When he joked with the officials, his
laugh was always loudest.  A lover of animals from his
youth on a Belgian farm, he raised great flocks of
chickens and pigeons; when he called them to be fed
they would fly to him and light on his head and shoulders.  Toward the end, after the period of depression
had passed, it was noted that once more he was seen
among the poultry, his shoulders covered with birds
while he stroked a chick in his hand.

There is a curious episode connected with this final
period, one that it is not easy to understand or explain.
His last letter was written to a Sister Ignatius in a
Belgian convent.  (Damien letters are rare, and they
command high prices when they are found; the existence of this one was not suspected until it came into
the market late in 1930.)  Brother Joseph was evidently writing for him, and this passage was added to
a longer communication:

"Do try to say a word to my brother P. Pamphile
and to my nieces.  They treat me as though they were
ashamed of my having caught this disease.  Through
nursing lepers I have become a leper myself, and I
strive to bear bravely this terrible burden that the
good God has kindly laid on me. . . . Tell P. Pam-

phile that I hope for a letter from him and the family
very soon."

Now Father Damien's family were never "ashamed"
of his disease—indeed had always looked on him as a
hero; and the passage is inexplicable.  It is true that
they may not lately have written to him; but it was at
this time that the European papers were carrying false
stories of his death, and the family may have accepted
these.

The various helpers who came to Molokai toward
the end of Damien's life have been mentioned—Father
Conrardy early in 1888, Father Wendelin later in the
year, the Franciscan Sisters in November.  The German priest Wendelin, who was to be Damien's spiritual successor, officiated at the funeral mass of the man
whose work he was to continue.  Wendelin remained
for fourteen years at Molokai, carrying out his duties
with mounting energy during that period.

Damien was able to go about until the early part of
March, 1889.  The effort must have exhausted him,
but he persisted in it.  On about March 9 there was a
sudden outbreak of open sores on his fingers that made
it impossible for him to say mass.  These, however,
seemed to heal within a few days, and once more he
was seen about the settlement.  But his end was at
hand, and soon he had to take to his bed, his restless
energy quenched at last; and after March 28 he did
not leave it again.  On the thirtieth he made his preparation for death.  Almost to the end his mind was

alert, and he showed his normal cheerfulness. On the day of the rites that looked toward his death he held out his hands to Father Wendelin with a smile. "Look, Father," he said, "at my hands. All the wounds are healing, and the crust is getting black. As you know very well, these are signs of death. Look into my eyes. I have seen so many lepers die that I cannot be mistaken. Death is not far off. The good God is calling me to celebrate Easter with Him."

On April 2 he talked of the future of the mission, contentedly now. "The work for the lepers is assured. I am no longer necessary to them; so before long I shall go up yonder." To this Father Wendelin replied: "Leave me your mantle so that, like Elisha, I may inherit your heart." There came kindly laughter from Damien's lips. "But what would you do with it? It's full of leprosy!"

He would not be kept in the house, but begged to be taken out into the open air. Here he lay for a while on a mattress; those who were taking care of him had difficulty in getting him to agree to lie in bed. Hourly the lepers thronged about the house, eager to see him, to speak once more to the priest who had fought for them. From the world outside, letters and gifts poured in, offers of aid from people who wanted to come and nurse him. Molokai was the focus of the world's attention now; it watched daily for news from Damien's bedside.

It had been Damien's hope that he might die before Easter, and his wish was to be granted. On the eve-

ning of Palm Sunday he suddenly lost consciousness.
When he rallied for a few moments he was given Holy
Communion for the last time.   Though he was a little
stronger the next day, his mind was wandering.   Once
in a while he would press the hands of those about
him, though without speaking.   On the fifteenth came
the end.   With a smile on his lips, as quietly as a child
dropping off to sleep, Damien died.

The long struggle was over.   The life that had
started on an obscure little farm in Belgium had ended
in an isolated colony of outcasts.   Humble in the beginning, at its close the eyes of the world were turned
upon it.   He had been an unknown and ill-educated
priest; he died a hero and a saint.

Damien was buried at the foot of the very tree beneath which he had slept for so many weeks when he
came to the Island.   This was his own choice for the
site of his grave.   He had written to his brother in
1880: "I was quite vexed the other day to find that
they had begun to dig a grave just in the very spot that
I had so long reserved for myself.   I had to insist that
the place be left vacant, since it was mine."   There is
a simple monument marking the spot, on one side the
words "Father Damien," on the other, "DAMIEN
DEVEUSTER."

At Kalaupapa, however, stands a nobler monument.
Not far from the steamboat landing, on the road now
called Damien Road, the English people have erected
a cross in the antique style of the 6th century, like
those found in the ruins of the seven churches of Clon-

macnoise on the River Shannon in Ireland.  On its pedestal are these words:

*The greatest proof of love man can
give is to give his life for his friends.*

More than this needed not to be said.  It was what Damien had done.

FATHER DAMIEN'S GRAVE BESIDE THE CHURCH AT KALAWAO

# CHAPTER VI

## VENOM

It may almost be said that the death of Father Damien did more for his lepers than ever his life had done. If the blood of martyrs be the seed of the Church, this martyrdom sowed the seeds of prosperity for the Molokai settlement. The chorus of praise that Damien's service elicited, especially in Europe and America, was at once turned to practical and concrete expression in money and help that was soon to make of the colony one of the most efficient medical centers in the world, and was to improve also the condition of lepers elsewhere.

The monument raised by the English has been mentioned. A more useful memorial grew out of the generosity that provided this. On July 13, 1889, *The Spectator* announced that such a memorial had been proposed; and so great was the public response that, with the Prince of Wales as patron, the "Father Damien Memorial Fund" was at once launched. Its objects were four. A monument was to be erected on Molokai; a fund raised to care for the lepers in England, of whom there were a few; an endowment was proposed for two scholarships whose holders were to study leprosy in China and the British colonies; and

finally a commission was to be sent to India to determine what could be done for the more than two hundred thousand lepers there at that date. All these
objects were effected.

But Damien's death had another consequence, the
attack on his memory by Dr. Hyde and the fierce rejoinder by Robert Louis Stevenson, a sensational affair
whose repercussions spread so wide that the details are
worth a chapter in our story. It is true that for one
person (outside the Islands) who knew of Damien's
work during his lifetime a thousand heard of it after
he died; but it is probable that still more were to learn
of it through Stevenson's eloquent tract in reply to
Hyde.

It was not until three months after Damien's death
that the first voice was raised in venomous attack,
through a letter printed in an obscure little religious
weekly published in Sydney, Australia. The writer of
this letter was the Rev. Charles McEwen Hyde of
Honolulu, who had come to the Islands under the
Board of Missions of the (American) Congregational
Church. He had been born in New York, graduated
at Williams College, and had charge of churches in
Massachusetts before coming to Hawaii in 1877. A
part of his work here was the management of a school
for training native pastors for mission churches. He
seems to have been something of a Puritan, strict, narrow, set in his ways, calm and unemotional by nature.
He moved among the social leaders of the Islands,
mostly the sons and descendants of missionaries who

had grown wealthy and who represented the financial and political power of Hawaii in that day.

Hyde visited the Molokai leper colony three times, his first visit being in September, 1885, for the purpose of consecrating a newly built Protestant church. He stayed for several days, looking at the schools and homes that Damien had established for the leper children. During this visit he expressed again and again his astonishment at the amount that had been accomplished and his admiration of Damien's work. He said—and Damien agreed with him—that the schools should be much larger and the buildings improved and modernized; and made what was for him a considerable admission—that trained nurses could never be got to the colony and that the Sisters and Brothers of Catholic societies were therefore the only kind of helpers possible, and were indeed the best fitted to do the work. For hours he talked with Damien, who gladly explained all the details of management and showed him every corner of the settlement.

On his return to Hawaii Hyde wrote a long description of this visit, which was published in the *Hawaiian Gazette*. In it he referred to Damien as "that noble-hearted Catholic priest, who went to Molokai in 1873 to care for the spiritual welfare of those of his faith, and whose work has been so successful." Note, then, that in 1885 he was praising Damien warmly, whereas four years later, when Damien had died, he repeated the foulest sort of slander about him. It is hard to understand this change, the only attempt at explain-

ing it being contained in a memorial to Hyde published by his son in 1901.  The son's explanation begins by saying that when his father first knew of Dami-
en's work he was filled with admiration.  But

"later he learned, from sources that could not admit
the shadow of a doubt, that some of his [Damien's]
personal habits were not all that could be desired.  He
mentioned these facts in a private letter, which his indiscreet correspondent put forth by publishing without his consent.  This letter called forth a violent
reply from Robert Louis Stevenson, and we are led to
believe that Stevenson saw this subject before his
death in a somewhat different light, and even said his
treatment of Dr. Hyde had laid him open to a very
heavy penalty.  That he ever retracted his letter or
modified its language we are not prepared to say, but
believe that he regretted its publication."

This defense of Hyde, however, carries us ahead of
our story.  The "private letter" mentioned was written in answer to a request from a Rev. H. B. Gage,
who had asked Hyde whether Damien was worthy of
all the honor that was being heaped on his memory.
Gage, on receiving Hyde's reply, had the bad taste to
send it for publication to the Sydney *Presbyterian;* and
it was this indiscreet action that generated the clash
between Stevenson and Hyde.  The letter is as follows:

"Honolulu, August 2, 1889.
"Rev. H. B. Gage.
"Dear Brother,—In answer to your inquiries about
Father Damien, I can only reply that we who knew the

man are surprised at the extravagant newspaper lauda-
tions, as if he was a most saintly philanthropist.  The
simple truth is, he was a coarse, dirty man, headstrong
and bigoted.  He was not sent to Molokai, but went
there without orders; did not stay at the leper settlement (before he became one himself), but circulated
freely over the whole island (less than half the island
is devoted to the lepers), and he came often to Honolulu.  He had no hand in the reforms and improvements inaugurated, which were the work of our Board
of Health, as occasion required and means were provided.  He was not a pure man in his relations with
women, and the leprosy of which he died should be
attributed to his vices and carelessness.  Others have
done much for the lepers, our own ministers, the government physicians, and so forth, but never with the
Catholic idea of meriting eternal life.

Yours, etc.,

C. M. Hyde"

At this distance of time it is possible to be sorry for
the Reverend Mr. Hyde; not that he thus revealed
how ill-informed he was; not that he betrayed a willingness to indulge in sidelong sneers at the Catholics;
not even that he put himself at the mercy of an injudi-
cious correspondent—but that the wide reaches of the
Pacific Ocean harbored at the time he wrote his letter
a man named Robert Louis Stevenson.  For Stevenson
not only knew the facts better than Hyde did; he was
a genuine lover of the good in his fellowmen—as Hyde
was not; and he could write the English language in a
way that Hyde could never have dreamed of.  The

result of his seeing the Hyde letter was the composition of a veritable masterpiece of honest invective.

But let us look first into the motives underlying
Hyde's charges.  The background that we must fill in
is the temper of Hawaii at the time.  There had been
much criticism of the wealthy and powerful position
of the descendants of Protestant missionaries, and of
the failure of their churches to do anything very constructive for the Molokai leper colony.  The Protestant churches at Molokai were put in charge of native
clergy, and the practice had had not very successful results, nor had these native clergy shown themselves so
energetic or so self-sacrificing as had Damien.  Now
jealousy has never been the exclusive prerogative of
the layman, and it is quite possible that something like
jealousy underlay the Protestant attitude toward the
priest during his lifetime—an uncomfortable realization of opportunity lost, of duty delegated to another.
Many of the articles written after Damien's death
about his work and the conditions at Molokai expressed wonder that the other churches had not shown
a like courage and devotion; and this criticism stung
because there was justice in it.  The opportunity was
there before them; they had the money and the ability
to meet it; and now they must stand by and see praise
showered on the Catholic priest—the lonely, handicapped fighter—who had met it.

As for Stevenson, he too knew the colony through
visiting it.  He had gone there in May, 1889, a few
weeks after Damien's death, and spent much time with

Brother Joseph Dutton, eager to learn all he might of
Damien's work through the man who knew most about
it. Dutton describes this visit in an unpublished
letter:

"Stevenson came. Remember his health seemed
poor; he was weak, and much depressed over it. Said
that Molokai was the most beautiful place he had ever
seen—restful, calm. Added had great mind to come
and spend the remainder of his years here. Said he
doubted if he would live long himself, and might as
well die here as anywhere. All this said on first night
on Island. Next morning he seemed more cheerful
and did not again refer to subject. . . . Asked many
questions about Damien, showing greatest interest in
all he did. Told him what I could, trying to give a
true picture of the sainted father. Felt deeply the sufferings of lepers, more so of children."

Those who love and admire R. L. S. may well wonder what would have been the consequences if he had
actually gone to live on Molokai. When we recall the
delightful memories of Vailima on Samoa, it is interesting to speculate on the differences that would have
been implied if he had lived out his days on the
Hawaiian Island instead.

Stevenson could never forget what he had seen at
the leper colony; again and again he spoke of it to
friends, and in the letter addressed to Hyde he speaks
of this visit in a significant sentence: *"Harrowing* is the
word." To him the figure of Damien was the figure
of a martyred saint—a saint with human imperfections,

true, but by the transcendent strength of his character
and the unexceptionable value of his service to humanity, a saint all the same.

During the following year—1890—Stevenson went to
Sydney.  As soon as he arrived someone asked him
whether he had seen Hyde's letter to Gage in *The
Presbyterian*.  One look at the letter, and Stevenson
exploded.  Mrs. Stevenson has described his mood as
he sat down to write his rejoinder.  He locked himself
in, composed his tract at one sitting, talked to himself
angrily as he wrote, tore his hair.  A thoroughly angry
man, Stevenson, that day!  So angry that he forgot all
about the danger of libel suits, intent only on rending
the author of what he considered a baseless slander on
a good man.

At this point we may examine Stevenson's own estimate of Damien, as formed after his conversations with
Dutton and subsequently set down in his diary.  Its
interest lies in the fact that, while he recognized the
characteristic Damien weaknesses, even made use of
some of the same epithets that Hyde had used, he yet
reveals a saner and sweeter judgment than Hyde's in
counterpoising these with Damien's greater virtues.
"A man of the peasant class," he called him, "shrewd,
ignorant and bigoted, yet with an open mind, . . .
superbly generous, essentially indiscreet and officious,
which made him a troublesome colleague, domineer-
ing. . . ."  It is conceivable, too, that the effect of
Damien's tragic death had dimmed in Stevenson's
memory the harsher aspects of the priest's character

and left chiefly the favorable impression he had got.
Yet the letter to Hyde none the less mentions frankly
the unpleasant traits as well as the pleasant ones.

This famous letter is now available to us in several
forms. Originally Stevenson sent it, on completion, to
London newspapers, which did not, however, care to
publish it on account of the likelihood of libel suits.
But *The Scots Observer* was less timid and published
the letter in two parts on May 3 and May 10, 1890.
Then the London publishers, Chatto & Windus, issued
it as an essay; but Stevenson refused to accept any roy-
alties. "The letter to Dr. Hyde," he wrote them, "is
yours, or any man's. I will never touch a penny of re-
muneration. I do not stick at murder; I draw the line
at cannibalism. I could not eat a penny roll that piece
of bludgeoning had gained for me."

The "bludgeoning" opens on a fiercer note than any
of us would expect from the gentle Stevenson we know
through his essays, his poems and stories, his warm and
friendly letters. What he thinks of Hyde is conveyed
promptly. He speaks of having been entertained in
Hyde's home in Honolulu some time before, but
"your letter to the Reverend H. B. Gage is a document
which, in my sight, if you had filled me with bread
when I was starving . . . would yet absolve me from
the bonds of gratitude. . . . I conceive you as a man
quite beyond and below the reticences of civility."
There is a good deal of this sort of thing in the intro-
ductory portion of the letter, relishable by those who
enjoy seeing a man hit out straight with no fear of

consequences when he knows his cause to be just. Then the charges made by Hyde are taken up one by one and answered out of Stevenson's own knowledge.

As we seek to balance the issues, try to look at each man's side, we realize two points that these antagonists had in common: both made erroneous statements, and both had had occasion to revise earlier opinions. Hyde had felt warmly toward Damien in 1885, only to condemn him out and out by 1889; and Stevenson's diary records adverse criticisms of the priest that he toned down considerably by the time he wrote to Hyde. Stevenson's mistake lay in asserting that Hyde had never visited Molokai, implying that he didn't know what he was talking about. But Hyde's errors were of a different sort, and Stevenson pounced on them all, even to the trivial point about the relative size of the settlement—that it was "less than half the Island" when, as Stevenson says, it was far smaller than this implies, more nearly a twentieth of the total area. As for Hyde's accusations, Stevenson treats them in two ways: either what is said is quite untrue, or it is true but is creditable to Damien rather than the opposite. In an earlier chapter we have taken up one of the latter kind of charges—namely, that Damien went "without orders." What if he did? All the more praise to him, in a day when it simply did not occur to anybody else to volunteer to enter the hell that was the Molokai leper settlement then.

Was Damien dirty? Stevenson asks. Well, this priest

had not been bred in the polite drawing-rooms of
Honolulu's rich folk; even if he had been, there were
no facilities for creating polite drawing-rooms on
Molokai—there was only filth, and disease, and lack of
the ordinary decencies of civilized life.   What order
was brought into the lives of those lepers, Damien
brought.   "There is not a clean cup or towel in the
Bishop Home, but dirty Damien washed it," Stevenson retorts.   And here we may begin to quote some of
the things that Brother Joseph said on the Hyde
accusations.

Three long statements have been left among Brother
Joseph's papers, dealing with various phases of
Damien's character and work.   Their dates are 1890,
1903, and 1905; the material in them will be liberally
drawn upon in succeeding chapters.   He speaks of the
charge against Damien

"to the effect that he was unclean in his personal
habits.  Of this I cannot say much in denial. When visitors were here he used to keep in presentable appearance, but ordinarily he paid very little attention to
cleanliness of person or dress.  He did not pretend to
be neat in his personal belongings.  He told me that
he considered this a defect.  He was very simple in his
bodily wants and was quite able to subsist upon the
coarsest fare."

Hear Joseph Dutton again on Damien's headstrong
ways—which nobody has ever denied, and which in-

deed seem to have been the very instrument by which the man got things done in the settlement that a milder person might still be waiting for.

"He was at times very vehement and excitable in regard to matters that did not seem right to him; or, if opposed by anyone, sometimes doing and saying things which he would afterward regret. But he had the faculty in a remarkable degree of putting resentment aside. Very soon after a heated altercation he would be toward the opponent as if no such thing had happened, seeming to have forgotten the incident. In certain periods he got on well with everyone. At all times he was urgent for improvements, or for what he thought were such. Father Damien had in his heart when tranquil—being moved neither by excitement nor by some absorbing purpose—a most warm, tender feeling, as I have often been made to know."

The passage in Hyde's letter that chiefly angered Stevenson was the one referring to Damien's sexual habits. The pages in which this charge is answered fairly sparkle with indignation. The story Stevenson tells about what once happened in a bar-room in Honolulu when somebody brought up this point is eloquent testimony to what was known about the real facts by those who were intimately acquainted with the priest. It is a temptation to quote Stevenson's answers on this as on other points; but the letter to Hyde should be read as a whole by those who are interested. There is now accessible further testimony, hitherto unpublished, that may preferably be given here, since it emanates from Damien's close associate, Brother Joseph.

"He was not a pure man in his relations with women," Hyde wrote, "and the leprosy of which he died should be attributed to his vices and carelessness." Now every authority today knows that leprosy cannot be contracted through sexual intercourse. But in Hyde's day the belief was common that it could be, and many a leper was accused of having taken the disease by this means. Indeed, a well-known physician of the time was responsible for another idea current in the Islands: he called leprosy the "fourth stage" of syphilis. The theory is of course not accepted now by the medical profession, nor was it at the time of Damien's death. But Hyde had probably heard of it, and evidently thought he was basing his accusation on a scientific fact. Yet, unscientific though it was, the charge constituted a direct attack on Damien's sexual morals that was based on no slightest shred of real evidence. What it was based on was the gossip of the lowest element in the life of the Islands—dissolute, lying natives, liquor-sellers and gamblers whom Damien had driven out of Molokai and who retaliated by spreading tales to his discredit. Nobody who knew conditions at the settlement as they really were took any stock in these tales, except those whom jealousy predisposed to credulity. And indeed there is one reputable witness whose testimony absolutely contradicts the suspicion of sexual irregularity. Dr. Mouritz, already mentioned as having been physician at

the colony, says that the women whose names were connected with Damien's were non-lepers—never contracted leprosy; a fact that evidently the fabricators
of this charge did not know.   He speaks, too, of having
been present when Damien was examined at the dis-
pensary at Kalawao, and quotes a pregnant remark of
the examining physician: "I want to examine him
especially for evidence of other disease."   And he satisfied himself that, though Damien was a leper, there
was nothing else the matter with him.   Throat, mouth,
and glands were examined carefully, and no trace of
any other disease was found.   The inference is that
the doctors had heard that Damien was alleged to be
suffering from venereal disease and—without saying
anything to Damien himself about it—wished to ascer-
tain the truth.   They did.

Let us see what Brother Joseph has to say on this
score.   We have in his handwriting the notes he made
from Damien's deathbed statement, notes signed by
the priest himself, and containing the clear statement:
"Never had any sexual intercourse whatever."
Brother Joseph writes of these notes: "This is a true
copy as signed by Father Damien.   I made the notes
from his own lips, using as nearly as I could his very
words, and read the statement all over to him before
he signed it. . . . The declaration as to non-sexual
intercourse was his own, voluntarily given."

Subsequently Dutton went more fully into the question, having evidently been asked for fuller information by the bishop after the Hyde story had been cir-

culated. From separate statements we bring together
here the relevant comments:

"In this connection it may not be out of place for
me to put upon paper what my own impression has
always been concerning Father Damien's chastity,
partly because of the question having been brought
up soon after his death in the public prints, and because it may possibly be brought up again. It is a
question one can never answer positively without
proof for support; therefore I can only state my own
impressions and belief. Regarding the remark that he
had never had any sexual intercourse, I would state
that he made it of his own motion and not from any
question or remark of mine, so far as I can remember.
There was not anyone present save Father Damien
and me. Why he made the statement (the absolute
truth of which, of course, I never doubted) was not
apparent to me. Idle remarks have been made against
Father Damien's chastity, but I never knew of any responsible source whatever, or of anyone who knew
anything about Father Damien who had any belief in
the tale. It might be that he had heard of the tale
himself and was suspicious that someone would take
it up after he died."

. . . . . . .

"The question of his purity has been brought up in
the public prints. I merely state my firm belief that
he was wholly devoid of sensuality during the time I
knew him. In going about the country it was sometimes necessary to stop overnight with natives. He
told me that one night when in one of these huts, a

young native woman being about to sleep near him, he left the house and stayed outdoors. It never occurred to me to question his lifelong adherence to virtue. He seemed, while I knew him at least, to have no thoughts of such things. The charges since his death are not new ones; I heard some while he was living. That is, the parties so informing me said that Father Damien was innocent of the charges except in so far as he apparently unwittingly gave grounds for suspicion by his want of caution in allowing women to be about his house, being apparently blind to what might seem evil in the eyes of others."

.    .    .    .    .    .    .

"He would wish the whole truth to be told, and if he had the selection of one to speak of his last years, he would, I think, certainly select me."

So far as we may ever arrive at "the whole truth," here, apparently, it is. Ira Dutton's style may be graceless, but his intention is unmistakably sincere; and the details furnished by his records confirm Stevenson's estimate. Even of the testimony of "Protestants who had opposed the Father in his life," Stevenson says that it builds up "the image of a man, with all his weaknesses, essentially heroic, and alive with rugged honesty, generosity, and mirth." Further— "Damien has been too much depicted with a conventional halo," and it was no part of Stevenson's intention to touch up that halo; but he wanted to see justice done.

Though the "Open Letter" brought instant and

wide publicity to Hyde's accusations, he did not at the
moment seek to reply to it, contenting himself merely
with this entertaining comment: "Stevenson is simply
a Bohemian crank, a negligible person, whose opinion
is of no value to anyone." As for the Molokai colony
itself he was said to have been instrumental later in
procuring some real assistance to it; it may have been
his influence that led two wealthy men of Hawaii to
make gifts that established orphanages for boys and
girls at the settlement. So creditable an act might enable us to overlook his earlier offense if he had not,
after a year had gone by, returned to the attack. On
August 7, 1890, he published a letter in the American
weekly, *The Congregationalist,* which had a wide circulation in the United States. In some respects it
was a more discreet letter than his first; in others, more
specific. "I have no desire," he writes, "to withdraw
or modify any statement formerly made." And he
proceeds to justify himself in an exquisitely illogical
argument. Commenting on Stevenson's admission
that Damien had come from the peasant class, and was
shrewd, ignorant, bigoted, and rough, he says: "I submit that such testimony from such a source, confirm-
ing what I have said of Father Damien, is presumptive
proof that I had equally good reason for saying what
else I said in regard to him."

If—that is—Damien washed none too often, that
proves that he was immoral. If he came from the
peasant class, that proved that his leprosy was the result of syphilis. If he was bigoted, then of course he

deserved no credit for having reformed conditions on Molokai. There is a certain charm in such a line of reasoning.

Hyde then makes a more specific attack, digging for himself a pit to fall into, a pit at whose bottom the unlucky man was to remain. "Before going to Molokai," he says of Damien, "he had charge of two other parishes, where it is believed he contracted the disease, and left behind him an unsavory repute." Here is a dirct allegation, easy to test, and the facts were readily discovered. As the time that Damien offered to go to the leper colony he was in charge of the parish of Kohala on Hawaii; and he was succeeded there by another priest. Now in 1880, some years afterward, this successor was accused of immorality, and the case went to the courts. Hyde's error lay in confusing the two men; and he came to know that he had done so. For when he learned that this statement was being challenged, he sought confirmation by writing to a Mr. E. C. Bond, the son of a former missionary, who lived in the parish of Kohala, asking for facts to bolster up the charge. But instead, what he got from Bond was a flat "You are wrong. You have mentioned the wrong man." Hyde wrote also to the superintendent of the leper colony: what had he to say about Damien's morality? And the reply to this was scathing. Yet even now, with not a leg left to stand on, Hyde made no move to retract; evidently he still had "no desire to withdraw or modify" what he had charged against his victim.

There are echoes of those charges even to this day,
and it is in the hope of stilling them finally that this
unsavory interlude has been included in our story.   It
may be ended with a mere sentence from Stevenson's
letter to Hyde: "For, if that world at all remember
you, on the day when Damien of Molokai shall be
named Saint, it will be in virtue of one work: your
letter to the Reverend H. B. Gage."

# CHAPTER VII

### A WISCONSIN BOYHOOD

UNDER the shadow of Mount Mansfield, the highest of the Green Mountains, lies the little town of Stowe, Vermont. Today the village is filled in summer with tourists, allured by the fine roads to seek the peaceful beauty of the hills. But in 1843 the roads were poor, Stowe was tiny, distant from the populous centers, and rather isolated from the world. On April 27 of that year there was born in the town a boy whose name, linked with that of Father Damien, was to become widely known. Ira, he was christened by his parents; but the world knows him better as Brother Joseph Dutton.

The Dutton family came of old English stock, their name being found in the Domesday Book. The original home of the family is near Chester, in Cheshire, and its ancestry has been traced back to a cousin of the Conqueror named Odard. The first Dutton emigrating to America arrived in New England in 1630, living first at Reading, north of Boston, and then at Billerica; whence his descendants scattered into New Hampshire, Vermont, and elsewhere. It was from the Vermont branch that Ira Dutton descended. In one of his letters he says that he knew nothing of his ancestry beyond his grandfather; though toward the close of his life he mentions having heard of the original family home in Cheshire.

For some hundred years before Ira's birth his family had tried to make a living by farming the rocky Vermont hills. His grandfather, Samuel, Jr., had a large family—ten children by his first wife, eight by his second. Six sons, all bearing Old Testament names, grew to manhood. Besides farming, Samuel Dutton had a trade; for, after all, Vermont farming was short in season and precarious in returns, and supplementary means of livelihood were imperative. In this family it was cobbling that was taught by father to sons; and the fourth son—Ezra, father of Ira—carried the family craft to Stowe, where he lived for eight years.

Of Samuel Dutton little is known. He was born in 1771 in Washington, Connecticut, and in his boyhood moved with his parents to Norwich, Vermont. He lived to be eighty-five, a quick, energetic man, much interested in local affairs and as religious as his father before him. His neighbors liked him, and spoke of his willingness to help the poor of the village. He called his farm "Dutton Hill," perhaps knowing that his family name comes from a Norman word meaning "village on a hill."

It was here that Ezra Dutton was born. "Know little about my father," wrote Ira. "He would never have a picture taken. Was fastidious in his dress, and in the care of his saddle-horse. Was modest, unassuming, and very devoted to his family. People liked him." It is rather remarkable that though Ira was thirty-six years old when his father died—at the age of seventy-seven—this is the only personal, intimate reference to Ezra Dutton that is to be found in the hundreds of his son's letters. The details of Ezra's life must be filled from other sources.

While still a young man Ezra Dutton left the family farm and went into the business of manufacturing potash and pearlash in the village of Stowe. He appears to have been successful in this venture, for when, a year after Ira was born, he decided to move again— this time to Taftsville, Vermont—he had a house as well as a business to sell. In Taftsville (a smaller town than Stowe) he was joined by his brother Noah in a shoemaking partnership. Again business must have been good, for they hired six men and kept them busy; at times they had eight working for them. The finer work on the shoes was always done by Ezra and Noah; their assistants were never allowed to cut the leather.

Shortly after going to Stowe—in 1831—Ezra married Huldah Darling. He was twenty-nine, his wife twenty-six. She died six years afterward, and is not mentioned in Ira's letters. A few years before moving to Taftsville Ezra married again, this time a country schoolteacher, Abigail Barnes, a woman of keen wit and considerable intelligence. Of her early life we know little. She was born in Rochester, Vermont, and was twenty-nine when she married. Like her husband she came from old New England stock, her ancestors having settled in the Plymouth Colony in 1637. Of this marriage four children were born: Ira in 1843, Ezra, Jr., in 1846, Owen in 1848, and Abigail in 1854. The second and the third child both died young; Abigail lived to be twenty-two.

If it is strange that Ira Dutton's letters refer only once, and briefly, to his father, surely it is no less strange that he makes no mention at all of his sister or his brothers. He seems indeed to have forgotten them. But he was never to forget his mother. "I suppose I was always what they call a mother's boy," he wrote. For years his mother was his only teacher; he never went to primary school. In later life when he was writing from Molokai he loved to repeat that she was "always teacher and chum"—the phrase appears in letter after letter. And it was his feeling for her that led him to adopt her maiden name, Barnes, as his own middle name.

"While a youth, out of deep affection and love for my mother I added a B. to my name—B. for Barnes, her family name. . . . A teacher before marriage, and my teacher when I was not at school, always my teacher and chum. So I was Ira B. Dutton then, and through the Civil War, and afterwards, until my fortieth birthday, when I became 'Joseph' Dutton."

Ira's father evidently had a restless streak in him, for he was to move once more, notwithstanding his successful business in Taftsville. Perhaps his wife persuaded him to go west; she had relatives in Janesville, Wisconsin, who often wrote to her, telling her how cheap farming land was out there and urging her and her family to move to the new territory. Here was wider opportunity, a new country; it would be easy for the Duttons to get along. Though Ira was never to be quite certain how old he had been when they went, we know that the date was 1847. Seventy-five years later, at Molokai, Brother Joseph collected pictures of his birthplace—Stowe—and mentions the town in his letters; but nowhere does he speak of Taftsville or of the journey westward.

Janesville at this date was passing through the history common to most frontier towns. When General Atkinson led his troops against the Sac Indians during the Black Hawk War, his enemies were encamped along the banks of the Rock River, near what was to be the site of the town of Janesville. After the war was over, the returning soldiers spoke of the beauty and the fertility of the Rock River valley; and presently—in 1835—two settlers from Pennsylvania journeyed there on a tour of inspection. They were joined by others, and by 1836 four families had settled along the river bank. When Ezra Dutton arrived with his wife and two children in 1847 the town was only twelve years old; but so rapid had been its growth that its population already numbered 1400.

The original settlers had for the most part been poor but adventurous folk of the pioneer type, seeking to make their fortunes or at least to better their condi-

ABIGAIL BARNES DUTTON, BROTHER JOSEPH'S MOTHER, AT THE AGE OF 77

tion in a new country. The Duttons, however, were in no sense pioneers. Ezra's shoe business had made money for him, and on arriving at Janesville he bought two houses. In one of these, on whose site the leading hotel of the city now stands, Ira spent his boyhood. Some years afterward the family bought a farm just outside the town; here Ira never lived, though it was his parents' home after the Civil War.

Of Ezra Dutton now we read that he was a quiet man, respected by his fellow-townsmen, and—for those times—fairly prosperous; his wife had domestic "help." Most of Abigail's time seems to have been devoted to her adored eldest. Though Ira was to live almost to the age of eighty-eight, he seems to have been delicate as a child. His mother indeed feared that he would die young; he did not, however, have any serious illness after he was six. They were much together, mother and son, dependent on each other; and Ira grew up a shy, sensitive child, averse to the rough play of other children and preferring to stay in the house reading, never wandering far from his mother's side.

His love of books was an early growth. Abigail Dutton implanted it successfully. Of four books only do we hear. "I read the Bible, 'Robinson Crusoe,' and 'The Pilgrim's Progress,' and my mother read me parts of Shakespeare," he wrote many years later. Not the worst literary fare for a youngster to begin on; perhaps the very soundest basis for that love of good books which was to last him through life. "Many times I sat close to my mother reading a book, when the laughter of my playmates outside drifted into the room."

Ira did not go to school until he was about twelve. "I fought against going to school." Daily his mother set aside a part of the morning for lessons with him, teaching him to read and write before he was five. And evidently her former experience as a teacher came in usefully, for when eventually Ira's father "dragged" him to Janesville Academy, he entered the high-school grade—on his first day in any school.

His own story of this first day suggests domestic discord. Thus far Ira had refused to go to school, and his mother had apparently backed him up. But by his twelfth year he no longer had the excuse of delicate health, being indeed a tall and sturdy youth. And so the hour came when Ezra Dutton insisted. Ira was too big a boy for further home teaching, and Ira was led by the hand through the streets of Janesville, pushed into the Academy building, and thrust willy-nilly into a seat. Ira never forgot this experience; perhaps it supplies the reason why he said so little about his father in after-years.

"The old Academy was the place where I first went to school. I say *went*, but that is hardly correct, at least as to the first day. Can remember that my father and Mr. Woodruff (the teacher) dragged me in, while I set my heels against everything, kicked and fought. . . . I don't know what it was that so set me against that school; but evidently it was very serious indeed. However, I went finally—had to, my father saying he would take me every day; and so in the end I went as all good boys do."

Later he attended Milton Academy, about eight miles from his home. He reports that "at the age of ten and a half" he had gone to work, but the available evidence suggests rather that he was twelve when he got his first job. It was no need of money that sent him after it, but largely a boyish ambition. "I supported myself from the time I was ten and a half, paid school expenses, bought my own clothes, and all. It was not a necessity, but my parents let me do this. Many young men and boys have some ambition. So did I." This hint of mental alertness and ambition was to be borne out in his after-life. The job itself was a part-time one, after school, on the *Free Press,* a Democratic newspaper that had just been started in Janesville; young Ira folded the papers before delivery. A friendship sprang up between the boy and the editor. "Old Mr. Baker began to call me his associate editor, and even put me in charge of a column called 'Fun.' " This column was not, of course, what today we call a "column" (or *colyum*), being merely an assemblage of clippings from exchanges. But that Ira was allowed even to do the clipping and the making-up bespeaks dependability. He was not to lose touch with this newspaper. "The daily paper still comes to me," he wrote, "from the place where I worked seventy-five years ago."

When he had been helping to edit the *Free Press*

for about a year and a half, working every afternoon and several evenings each week, he had the offer of another job. "James Sutherland's Book Store—Wallpaper, Books, Stationery, and Binding" is still in existence, with a long and interesting history that makes it one of the oldest bookstores in America. In Ira's boyhood it was the leading store of its kind in the town, and the boy often halted before its windows to study the display of current books and to long for a job inside. Now, when it was offered to him, he took it promptly.

He was still in school, but here again he worked in his spare time, including Saturdays and vacations: first in the bindery, for six months; then in the wall-paper department down on the first floor; and then in three months came promotion to selling books to the public. Mr. Sutherland is quoted by his son as having said of Ira that "he was the best clerk I ever had." No matter what style of letter-paper was called for, or what book, Ira knew where to find it. And every day he was going to Milton Academy, driving eight miles each way. By the time he was graduated at eighteen he was offered a full clerkship and accepted it.

What were the books that young Ira Dutton wrapped up for his customers in the late '50's? Dime novels probably; he speaks of having read these, and it was in 1860 that the Beadles published their first "dollar book for a dime"—"Malaeska" is title and Ann Sophia Winterbotham Stephens its author. The store carried magazines, too: *Godey's Lady's Book, Peter-*

*son's National Ladies' Magazine, The Independent, Harper's, The Atlantic Monthly.* And among the (so to speak) legitimate novels he mentions "The Marble Faun," "Pickwick Papers," and "The Mill on the Floss." But it was not a fiction-reading period, though "Uncle Tom's Cabin" was approved by the orthodox. Most of the books that young Ira handled were, it is to be feared, dreary religious works now long consigned to deserved oblivion. But the boy read them all—or so, at least, it seemed to him when he recalled his bookstore career from a distance of seventy years.

He followed enthusiastically the fads of his generation, notably the collection of autographs; not the autographs of the great, but those of one's friends, who must inscribe their names, with appropriate sentiments, in the fat album whose size and costliness measured one's social standing. Ira's album was a very special one, in which he took real pride because he had made it himself. We may picture him working in odd moments in the bindery above the bookstore, planning and executing the design which was to give him what he wanted. "You could not buy one so solid as mine. I made it of heavy material. My only help was one man, the bookbinder. He did the tool-work in finishing the cover, and it was by far the most beautiful as well as the heaviest autograph album in Janesville." Proud boy! He gave the album away when he went off to war, but he never lost the memory of it. From Molokai he writes of having used parchment for some of the leaves. This was a gift from a Norman Wiard. "Mr. Wiard came in and gave me a parchment for the book, saying that it was the bottom part of a patent issued to his father. It bore the signatures of John Quincy Adams, President; Henry Clay, Secretary of State; and William Wirt, Attorney-General, as I recall now. I gave the book away, and this page was in it. I wonder where it is today. It would be worth something." It would indeed.

Another of the boy's hobbies was coin-collecting, and his collection passed into the hands of the father of one of his friends. "The coins I gave Col. Lyon's father, a lovable old gentleman and a great bug-collector—insects and all such things which never interested me." He does not seem ever to have collected stamps.

There are other details told of Ira Dutton's boyhood, most of them probably apocryphal. We do not really know a great deal about these years, for it was half a century before he took to recalling them himself, in letters to friends, and even here there are great gaps—"secret years" he calls them, whose incidents he never mentioned. Stories that, in various published accounts of his early life, tell of his having worked as a printer, or a clerk in a drugstore, or in a railroad office, may be rejected as untrue. One of his relatives, Ethel R. Simmons, whose mother was a friend of Ira's in their childhood, "knows more about my early life and history than I do." She writes that he never did any of those things while he lived in Janesville. But we learn that he had three chief enthusiasms: in his spare time (of which he cannot have had much) he played at gymnastics, was a volunteer fireman, and acted as librarian.

Just before the Civil War a wave of interest in physical culture spread through the country, in due course reaching the Middle West. The Janesville Gymnastic Club was formed; Ira Dutton, a charter member, was elected secretary, and the first meetings were held with great enthusiasm. Then it dawned on the club—so the story runs—that though they had a hall, and plenty of eager members, what was really needed before they could start operations was somebody to tell them what they were to do. There was no trained leader, nobody who knew anything about gymnastics. And the thing seems to have expired prematurely, with Ira Dutton left holding the key of the hall but with no money to pay the rent. Yet evidently the "club" was not quite dead, but merely translated; it turned itself incontinently into "Zouaves." This was the name being given in various places to semimilitary organizations with irresistible uniforms. And soon Janesville, too, had its Zouaves, and again the good-looking Ira Dutton was made secretary. One sees him in his red trousers and jaunty cap playing at being a soldier, and basking in the admiration of pretty girls in the scoop-bonnets and swaying hoopskirts of the period. This playing at war was not to be wasted, for not long afterward came war's stern reality. The training that the Zouaves received was probably crude, but Ira said in after-years that his gymnastic work—what there was of it—and the training he had had with the Zouave Cadets were distinctly helpful to him in his army life.

Then there was the State Historical Society, of which Ira was to remain a member as long as he lived. It had been formed shortly after the Duttons moved to Janesville, and when the boy was about twelve he won the warm friendship of the man who had organized it, Lyman C. Draper.

"Must have had an early bent toward historical curios. Became possessed of an Indian prayer-book while a boy in the bookstore. . . . This book became one of the early items in the new library just started by the Historical Society. By some means Mr. Draper and I became good friends, though I do not remember ever meeting him. This prayer-book, given to his society, was the means of the friendship starting. His letters were among my early treasures, and the Society reports were the basis of my infant library."

Another organization that Dutton joined was to bring him excitement as well as pleasure. As soon as he was old enough he became a member of a Janesville volunteer fire company. There was no paid fire department in the town, and the various volunteer companies developed a healthy rivalry. Ira belonged to the "East Side No. 2 *Water Witch* Engine Company," the largest of the four, with fifty-seven members. When the fire-bell rang out its warning there was always a rush of amateur fire-fighters—every member dropped his work and dashed to the station, and each company tried to be the first on the job. The result sometimes was that the firemen fought each other instead of the fire.

Once a year the whole town turned out to watch the firemen's parade. Flowers decorated the engines— they were of the old-fashioned type with pump handles on each side—and the members strained at the ropes as they marched along the streets carrying their brass trumpets. There were prizes for the best decorations, and at the end the annual competition to see which engine could throw the longest stream of water. One year Ira Dutton marched in the parade as torch boy; the next year he had earned the honor of pumping at the handles of his engine in the effort to win the prize for his company.

Such authenticated episodes are a little hard to reconcile with that other clear picture of the boy that has come down to us from various contemporary sources. His friends speak of him as shy, quiet, reserved, not given to conversation or gayety, and making few close friends. Fifty years later one of his contemporaries described him as "a boy clean in speech and deportment, a great lover of home, and never very far from his mother, who was his teacher and constant companion. He had few friends, was very reserved, and took no part in the activities of other youths." Yet that shyness must have broken through at some period, or worn off with the years, for no friendless lad ever became a member of a crack fire company. Membership in these was not merely a civic right; it indicated popularity and social prestige of a sort.

Yet he must have been fundamentally a serious and thoughtful boy, responding willingly to the religious influences that were traditional in his family. Both father and mother were devout church-goers, and the boy was taken to Sunday School from the time that he learned to walk. Indeed, he seems to have gone to two Sunday Schools. According to Miss Simmons, who quotes her mother's reminiscences, "From early childhood Ira attended Sunday School with interest and regularity. Most of the time he went to the Baptist school, but there were times when he also attended the Methodist. In both he gave evidence of remarkable ability in memorizing Bible verses; and in both Sunday Schools he acted as librarian." We must conclude that one church held Sunday School in the morning, and the other in the afternoon; and also that it must have taken some little tact—in that day of sectarian intolerance and animosity—to keep in the good graces of both the Baptists and the Methodists. As eleven-year-old librarian it was his duty to hand out the pious inanities that in that age passed as proper Sabbath reading. He also taught a Sunday School class at various times—one of boys, another of young women.

But his placid life was to be interrupted before he entered manhood. War was clouding the horizon.

Every night now the Zouaves drilled. Feeling ran
high, and Janesville had scant sympathy for the Southern cause. Ira Dutton took his military drilling in
dead earnest, even asking for time off from the store
to attend the meetings. By the summer of 1861 the
date when he was to become a real soldier was in sight.
Almost all of the Zouave Cadets were going, and it
was with them, in Company B, 13th Regiment, Wisconsin Infantry Volunteers, that Ira enlisted on September 9. His certificate of service records him as
having blue eyes, light hair, and fair complexion, and
being five feet seven inches tall; his occupation,
"clerk." Then came the farewell reception for him
given by his Sunday School class. We may quote the
*Janesville Gazette* for October 2:

"The members of the Baptist Sunday School, especially his class, presented to Mr. Ira Dutton, who for
some years has been their librarian and who is about
to leave for the War with the Zouave Cadets, a valuable rubber overcoat and a Bible. The pastor made
the presentation speech, expressing the universal feeling that he would prove as faithful as any in the Army,
as faithful as he had been in the Sunday School; and
that all would be proud of him. The speaker said that
the school would follow him with their prayers, and
that he was going to fight for the children and those
who could not go; that he was offering himself on the
altar of a noble cause and that, God on his side, he
would be shielded from danger and immoral influences. There were many moistened cheeks in that

assembly, and earnest prayers ascended in behalf of the young volunteer."

It seems that Ira acknowledged these sentiments with a speech, but if so it has not come down to us. Nor do we know very much about his actual departure from Janesville, which was to come a few weeks after the reception. "An exciting time," he calls it himself, writing in 1924. "Streets lined with cheering crowds, bands playing, flags flying"—all the "glory," evidently, with which boys have always been sent off to the battle-field. Some sweetheart—her name forgotten—rushed out from the sidewalk as Ira marched by and pressed into his hand an ambrotype of herself. This he carried with him for three years, only to have it taken when the enemy captured his baggage in Alabama in 1864.

One thing, however, we may be sure of; it is not overworking our historical imagination to include Ira's mother in the host that gathered at the station to see the boys off. Her face was doubtless the last sight he looked on as the train pulled out. But it was to be a long time before he saw it again.

The Boys of '61 knew no such phrase as "the long, long trail." But for one of them—for Ira Dutton—the trail he was setting forth on, that autumn day, was to wind long and far. For he was not going to war only; he was going out into a life that was to be a pilgrimage. The Civil War was only an incident in it. The trail had begun in a quiet little village in the Green

Mountains of Vermont; it was to end on an island in the Pacific Ocean, in a grave not far from Father Damien's.

# CHAPTER VIII

## FIGHTING IN THE CUMBERLAND

ONE of the less intolerable aspects of warfare is the way it develops latent leadership. Ira Dutton was an example of this process. His character as a boy gave no hint of what he was to become as Father Damien's helper and successor. His self-reliance, his initiative, his ability to get willing service out of others, all were the product of his experiences in the Civil War. These were remarkable for no particular glory; indeed, he saw little actual fighting. But the facts disclosed in the papers he left are worth examining for the light that they throw, indirectly, on the indubitable power of leadership that he displayed afterward in the management of the leper colony.

On September 9, 1861, Ira Dutton left the bookstore and walked down the street to enlist for a term of three years in the 13th Regiment of Wisconsin Infantry. Company B, to which he was assigned, was made up largely of young men whom he had known all his life, and included many of the Janesville Cadets. Its first captain was Edwin Woodman, who had been captain of the Janesville Zouaves. These had voted to enlist as a body, and Woodman, who was principal of one of the schools and had taught most of the boys, resigned his position and enlisted with them. On October 17 the company was mustered into service.

The 13th Regiment was a local organization, drawn from the surrounding country, and had plenty of enthusiasm. But it was deficient in training. The cadets and similar groups from other towns had been drilling for some time; but except for these the recruits were quite unskilled in the use of arms. The regiment therefore went at once to Camp Tredway to begin drilling. This camp was not far from Janesville, on a high, bleak prairie. Once there, the soldiers promptly encountered many of the hardships that untrained troops must expect.

The quartermaster's department had its share of these, and it was to this department that young Dutton had been assigned. Nine days after having been mustered in, he was appointed quartermaster-sergeant and transferred to the non-commissioned staff. The responsibility involved was a rather heavy burden for eighteen-year-old shoulders, but they seem to have broadened under it as time went on. At home he had been regarded, apparently, as a shy and rather friendless boy; what lay beneath was to be brought to the surface by military responsibilities and made dominant for the rest of his life.

Within a week after the regiment entered camp an epidemic of measles swept its ranks. The hospital tents overflowed with patients; the quartermaster's department worked night and day building wooden huts, rushing supplies, trying to resolve order out of the inevitable chaos. It had been expected that the regiment would leave the bleak, wind-swept camp before winter should set in, but the epidemic prevented this. And winter came earlier than usual that year, as if to show the recruits at the very beginning of their service that war was no lark. Again and again the thermometer dropped to 25° below zero, and the snowdrifts piled high. At this elevation the cold winds beat upon the thin army tents, and fires were built and kept going. One of Dutton's first duties was to provide the wood for these fires—great quantities of four-foot cordwood—so that they might burn night and day. It was not until January 18, 1862, that the regiment was in fit condition to break camp and start for the war area. This was a momentous event for the boy; he told a comrade, a few hours later when they were marching through Chicago, that it was the first time he had ever been away from home.

Of the new kind of life that he was to encounter for the next three years we know little except what official records tell us; in his own papers that life seems to have been overshadowed by the significant events of his later missionary service. "When I came here," he wrote in 1907 at Molokai, "I promised myself to restrict as far as possible or expedient all letter-writing. This I observed for twenty years." And in the letters that he did write, after that time, we find only scant reference to his army experience, though many of them were written to former army comrades. For our knowledge of what happened to him and what he was

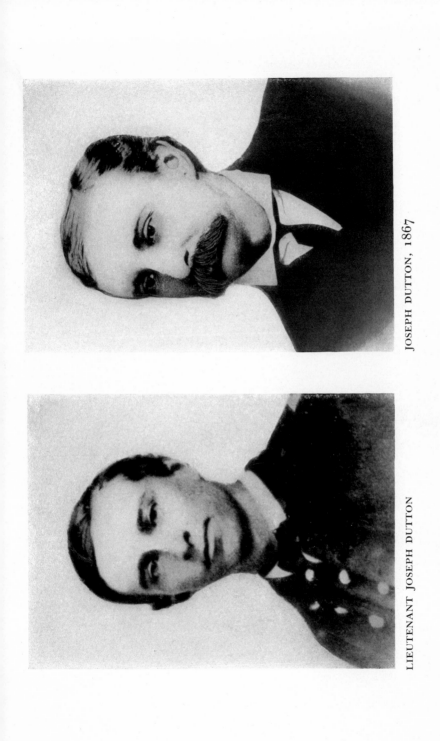

JOSEPH DUTTON, 1867

LIEUTENANT JOSEPH DUTTON

like during those three years we must largely depend
on other sources.

Dutton's regiment was not to be used in many of
the important actions of the War.  It was later alleged
that this fact was due to favoritism—that political influence spared the 13th from the hard fighting that fell
to other units.  But this represents the situation un-
fairly: the truth is that the function assigned to the
13th usually was that of holding positions that other
units had won—not an unimportant job, since often
the loss of such a position would have brought disaster.
The 13th was part of the Army of the Cumberland,
whose service lay in the western area of activity along
the Tennessee River.  Lookout Mountain, Missionary
Ridge, Chickamauga, and Sherman's march to the sea
—with all these the 13th was associated; though it took
no active part, being kept on garrison and picket duty
holding positions already gained.  For instance, toward the end of December, 1862, Forrest's raiders,
whose guerilla warfare had been making trouble, were
hunted down in a long pursuit, which ended in his
being defeated near Corinth and losing most of his
artillery.  Again, when Hood determined to take
Nashville and thus prevent Sherman's plan to march
to the sea, it was Ira Dutton's regiment that balked
Hood's attempt.

But to return to his introduction to army life.  One
of his letters reports first that on leaving Chicago they
traveled in comfortable trains to Quincy, Illinois,
where they marched across the Mississippi River.  As

quartermaster-sergeant it was his duty to see that the supplies and baggage got across safely. And at Quincy he "had first insight into what might happen. Here regiment left train, to cross river to cars on other side. The river was covered with ice—thin, unsafe. Men crossed at intervals of ten feet, got all over safely. Baggage more of a problem. Found an open space in river lower down, and took it over in boats. An exciting experience."

During the rest of January and the early part of February, 1862, the regiment was quartered in buildings at Fort Leavenworth, Dutton's department being engaged in outfitting the regiment for its journey of 130 miles to Fort Scott. Then on February 7 the men began their first long march, just after a heavy snow and sleet storm. The roads were covered with ice, and the going proved almost impossible for the supply wagons. Though later Dutton was not often to fail the men who depended on him for supplies, he did so on the first day of this march. The wagons loaded with blankets and tents, though drawn by six mules each, failed to reach camp by nightfall; and the next morning the 13th, fortified by whisky, straggled out over icy roads after a bitter night passed in the open. Such difficulties with the wagons are illustrated in a description—from one of Dutton's letters—of the crossing of the Kansas River: "Every wagon had a chain and a heavy rope attached to hind axle. We dropped them down the steep banks, with the men holding back on the ropes. Only one wagon upset; and after

we had crossed the ice and reached the other side, I
gave a sigh of relief."

Fourteen days it took them to reach Fort Scott, and
here they stayed until March 26. Then came orders
that made the men grumble: they were to go on to
New Mexico, and they had to march 150 miles of the
way. But they were marching better now, learning
how to become soldiers; and the quartermaster corps
was running more smoothly. They covered the 105
miles from Lawrence to Fort Riley in seven days—and
then were ordered to return to Fort Leavenworth.

Not until May 29 did the 13th at last begin to approach the theater of war. They had been away from
Janesville for five months, and not a shot had been
fired at the enemy. But after they had been made
the garrison of Fort Donelson they had their first real
skirmish, when, on an expedition to Clarksville, Tennessee, they were ambushed by a force of 900, which
they defeated.

For some months thenceforth they were engaged in
sudden scouting dashes into the country and in watching the movements of the guerilla raiders. Forrest
was always bothering them, cutting in and out of their
lines, until they caught him at Corinth. Between
scouting, fighting the raiders, and preventing any
movement up the river, they were kept busy well
through the summer of '63.

As for young Dutton, now nearly twenty years old,
he was commissioned second lieutenant of Company I
in February, 1863, and ordered on special duty in

the quartermaster's department.  In July he became
acting quartermaster of his regiment, and served thus
until April, 1864, when he was placed on special duty
with a district outside of Nashville under his control.
By now he was no longer a sensitive, shy boy, but was
showing some of the qualities of a leader.  One of his
generals called him "the handsomest fellow I ever
met, and one of the bravest and best officers in the
Army.  He could do anything."  There seems to have
been a good deal of the daredevil in him, predisposing
him equally to prank or to duty.  Officers and men
liked him, and he was able to get good work out of
even the most ordinary men; they would work harder
for him than for anyone else.  His superiors gradually threw more and more responsibility on him.  Another officer said of Ira Dutton as quartermaster:
"He had a rare gift for business, was quick, accurate,
and courteous, and handled the work with satisfaction.
There was no more efficient man in the Army."

One of the letters mentions the move of June, 1864,
when the lines of the Army of the Cumberland were
advanced into northern Alabama.  "I was assigned as
quartermaster of the expedition, General R. S.
Granger in command.  The headquarters were established at Decatur above Muscle Shoals.  I was made
post quartermaster at Decatur, and later quartermaster
of the district also.  District about 50 miles by 150."

It is of this period in his service that he was later to
write the longest account—in a 26-page letter from
Kalawao in May, 1907.  He is discussing the value of

fortifying the Hawaiian Islands, and suddenly begins to recall his experiences during the latter part of the Civil War. This constitutes the most valuable, as well as the longest, document we have covering this part of his life. He begins with a reference to the dashing cavalry leader Forrest, a unique and capable soldier who was forever raiding the Union lines of communication and turning up in the least expected places. Ira Dutton betrays something like admiring affection for this foe.

"Once I outfitted Confederate General Forrest's force quite nicely—with uniforms and about twenty-five carloads of supplies that should have reached our regiment holding the Tennessee River between Chattanooga and Decatur. The uniforms being blue instead of gray was no objection. General Forrest's forces needed anything they could get at that time. They could get and did get a good many things from us at one time or another, and gave us lots of trouble [by] getting through our supply lines. He was a 'wizard of the saddle,' and I did outfit him well this one time.

"I know something about military construction. From 1861 to 1865 we had a system of blockhouses and earthworks—little houses built of logs and covered with earth—along the hundred and fifty miles of river and two hundred and forty miles of railroad. Built most of them. With Forrest's raiders dashing everywhere at any time, and General Roddy's Confederate force lying just a little south of us, it was not just like falling off a log to keep those stations supplied; and that was my work, it had to be done, they depended on me. The cavalry detachments were scattered everywhere, and I had to supply them as well as find them. Besides using the railroad lines, an armed transport was turned over to me. The *Stone River* it was, largest steamer above Muscle Shoals, and I managed to keep this boat foraging along the river.

"General R. S. Granger (the Regular) was in command. I was quartermaster on his staff. Also post quartermaster at Decatur, Alabama. The troops holding these lines—river and rail—were supplied from there by me. I was allowed to construct and carry on general repair shops and keep extensive supplies of all sorts—usually for 15,000 troops; also put a pontoon bridge across the river. Decatur was on the south side. I say *was,* for two considerable cities [are] there now. When we reached there, 1864, two main residences and a small hotel were the only things left running. I used most of the rest of the town for my supplies, stores, stables—everything.

"Hood tried to get my pontoon bridge on his Nashville raid. Could have got it. But he made a terrible blunder then, and lost his chance for quick arrival before Nashville. The defense of Decatur was one of the most wonderful things for the War. Our main force was scouting, and Forrest was known to be up to some of his pranks. We did not think of Hood at all. I myself was dodging Forrest, rushing supplies from Nashville, and bringing money down to pay civilians. Once he almost got me when I had $22,000 on me. I was busy all hours, had soldiers detailed and men working. When news came of Hood's being before us, I hurried to Chattanooga with orders for all the transports on the river—eight; getting all the rolling stock moving, about twenty trains in all, and wagons— had 500.  We got them through; terribly risky thing. And Col. Prosser put all our small force out on skirmish line, thinking Hood would not know actual condition.  And Hood, always so reckless as a rule, was slow for once; waited until we had plenty of men and taking Decatur was out of the question.  When Hood learned the true facts—that he had failed his chance— [I] think he lost all hope.  If we had failed, War would have lasted at least a year longer.

"You see, Thomas had taken best of Army to march with Sherman through Georgia, and Rousseau had the rest of it with him on a raid in Alabama.  I outfitted his force fully.  When General Rousseau noted that I had gotten about 400 extra men, and fresh horses, and twenty trains of supplies ready, and all properly distributed and outfitted, he asked General Granger to let me go with him as quartermaster; but he would not.

"But I must not take all the credit for saving Decatur!  Must tell of my men.  We were then sent to try and bag Hood's retreating remnants.  Evacuated Decatur, destroyed the bridge and [what] supplies we could not move; we did not have to destroy very much.  We worked everything to the limit.  The property loss was only $105,000, and in his annual report the Quartermaster-General treated my work as a successful movement.  It was—we all of us had much praise.  The official praise all came to me, of course. But no one can do things without men, and I had a

fine force of excellent men—trained and tried. I
picked them mostly. It was rather notable, was rather
a saying: if any difficult thing, or thing out of the ordinary, was on hand, better give it to Dutton—he has
men who can do anything. So it was the men mostly,
and my luck in having them.

"My chief clerk was double my age—wanted it so.
Had one hundred citizens of all sorts, besides mechanics and the Regulars. Used most of the citizens
as scouts. They were [made] footloose by the War,
willing to learn and earn. I used them in foraging,
and paid them. I also had a spy—a young woman
named Miss Mitchel; she did much. Many mechanics,
who all came from northern cities, often men who took
such steps to keep out of the Army and at the same
time got good pay for working. They were generally
competent, but they were not wishing to go so far
south as Alabama. They liked to work in the larger
posts, like St. Louis, where they could have the
pleasure of going at a rapid pace. And things were
going at a rapid rate in the line of pleasure in those
days.

"The time I had the largest force was when we had
finished bagging Hood. But this bagging was like
snipe-shooting—holding the bag only; for he went the
other way, back as he came, and was nearly destroyed.
After going back to Decatur the troops were deployed
as before along the river and railroad. It was a time
of hustling on all sides, and in deep red mud, awful
mud, with little shelter. It could not be helped—we
were all in mud, and construction work was for the
purpose of getting out of mud and having warehouses

for supplies. I put sawmills in operation all over north Alabama. At Decatur my department had quite a job—to make pontoon boats, and relay the bridge, and put up buildings. Overhauled the sawmills in the district, got loggers, sawmill men, logging teams, all machinery wanted. Built a cordwood road of about three miles to a mill. As the logs were hauled in, my sawyers got the lumber out at once. It was sent over the pontoon to Decatur. The building was going on, and we tried to make allowances for the green lumber. Had good shingles. In thirty days and nights had put up a two-story office building, four houses, a warehouse 90 by 90 feet, a wagon shop 120 feet long, a blacksmith shop with six fires, a paint shop, saddler's shop, stables, sheds, wagon-yards, and places to keep thousands of horses and mules.

"In these two years I was twenty-one and twenty-two years of age, one of the youngest officers in the Army of the Cumberland on the field having considerable responsibilities—perhaps the youngest. After the surrender of Lee, I was selected to be in charge of Cumberland River transportation and the Nashville Depot transportation. I don't remember the number of boats on the Cumberland, but I believe I had about 2,000 teams and wagons, and perhaps 5,000 horses and mules. Had been before this commissioned first lieutenant and quartermaster of the 13th Regiment.

"But the Fourth Army Corps, under General Stanley, my regiment being a part, was at San Antonio, Texas, taking a little look over the Rio Grande into Mexico, all under General Sheridan in command at New Orleans. I wished to rejoin my regiment and

obtained orders for that. At New Orleans, waiting a
few days for a vessel that could take my two saddle-
horses to Galveston, I took some letters addressed to
him [Sheridan] at his headquarters. The affair in
Mexico was settled, and most of the volunteer regiments were to be mustered out. General Sheridan
published an order putting me on duty in New Orleans
to await my regiment. Was assigned as assistant to
Col. Holabird, Chief Quartermaster's Department of
Louisiana. This was the fall of 1865. I had been in
the field all the time, and this was my first gilt-edged
duty. I was mustered out in January, 1866.

"This covers about one-third of my military service
—that is, in the War. The whole was about four years
and four months. I was with the Zouaves before the
War for two years, and after the War was employed
by the War Department for ten years. I have never
written this before—it's rather a recent thing for me
to talk any about the War. Up to a short time ago I
seldom spoke about it. But [I] have told all that is of
interest."

Dutton was never wounded, nor did he have a single
day of illness throughout the War. His memory of
the service, he says, "is gratifying. Slept often on
ground, several times on ice and snow at the start,
but never missed duty and was never sick a day." In
1863 he had a slight accident in which his foot was
injured; of this he wrote late in his life—in 1920—:
"What just put me in bed was the return of a foot and
ankle difficulty that began with an accident in 1863

in camp. It quickly healed and for fifty years was a good boy. . . . About five years ago there was a small reappearance by reason of some strain, and now again; but it is about over."

Though the 13th Regiment was ready to return to Wisconsin, Dutton did not go with it; but he was able to do his comrades a service. It was part of his duty to arrange transportation for the demobilized troops. "At the muster-out of the regiments after the Mexican affair with France closed, it was a busy time for me, assigning the regiments to boats on the river transport fleet." He did not forget his own unit, securing for their use the *Ruth,* at that time the best boat on the Mississippi; so that they returned home in ease and luxury instead of being forced to use an ordinary stock steamer, overcrowded and in poor condition. We are told that Dutton went down to the levee to see his comrades start their long journey up the river; his uniform was the last one they saw as the boat headed northward. He had not been home since enlisting in 1861; for when, during the War, the other men's enlistments ran out and they returned to Wisconsin to reenlist, he had not gone with them. And now it was to be long before he would see Janesville or his family again. Only once did he ever return, and then for a few days only. The explanation of this is not known. He loved his mother with a deep and tender love throughout his life; but he never—excepting this once—went to see her.

It may be that a record such as this was not uncommon among the very young boys who enlisted in the Civil War; but it is none the less potent to evoke a thrill of wondering admiration. Think of the manifold responsibilities, the difficulties so alien to his previous experience, that were thrust upon this lad in his teens. What a record of trustworthiness, level-headedness, ability to get along with men under him and men over him, in the four or five years before he was twenty-two! It raises questions that cannot be answered: where, for instance, did he get the expert practical knowledge of building and railroad construction, where his efficiency in handling large groups of men? Not in a Janesville bookstore, certainly. Even the most hightly skilled contractors today hardly face much greater tests of their mechanical ability than did young Dutton in his unremitting efforts to keep the lines of communication open for his regiment at Decatur. Under his direction large numbers of bridges, roads, blockhouses, and railroads were planned and constructed. Besides the mechanical problems involved, there must have been human problems—friction, slacking, dereliction of duty. Yet his official record bears no hint of incompetency or failure. He may have gone into the War in 1861 a shy, inexperienced, self-mistrustful boy; but it is evident that when he came out of it four years later he was an able manager of men, confident of his ability to tackle any job that came to him. If our last quotations from his letters sound the note of pride, it is but a natural and honorable pride.

"I received much praise for my military record. Officers, many of whom I have lost sight of, speak in terms of high praise and great affection—the praise being rather overdrawn, I think. Each one speaks of my being complimented for bravery. But I thought it better to put down my larger responsibilities; in these I think there was special credit, considering my age—or youth, rather. As for personal bravery, I don't entirely disown some little mention of it, but I don't consider it very important."

And towards the end of his life he recalled another incident with pride. He wrote in 1926:

"Toward the close of the War [I] was quartermaster of brigade, having charge of District of Northern Alabama; the money and property responsibilities in these assignments being estimated at twenty million dollars. After the close of the War [I] was given by the Department at Washington a clean certificate of non-indebtedness. I was [at this time] 21 and 22 years old. Years later I heard that there was a credit in my favor at Washington of $600. Never claimed it. My country owed me nothing. I had been well repaid for anything I ever did. I should feel ashamed to take anything, for I am indebted to my country."

# CHAPTER IX

## THE SECRET YEARS

If Ira Dutton had not put off writing a letter for one week, the history of the leper settlement after Damien's death might have been very different; the young soldier's life would have turned into a channel that might conceivably have carried him to any other part of the world instead. For as the Civil War drew to a close he was considering applying for a commission in the Regular Army, and he would have had it if he had not waited a week to make up his mind to send in the application. "It was tolerably well known," he says, "that there were expectations concerning the Regular Army for me, with kind words from four Major Generals." And elsewhere:

"There was a special complimentary appointment just before [I was] mustered out, as Captain and A.Q.M., the duties of which I had performed for more than a year. It had been recommended by Generals Thomas, Donaldson, Rousseau, and Granger. But the number authorized had been filled, so this complimentary appointment was made just before muster-out. Two companies of my regiment at San Antonio, Texas, were soon to be 'captainless,' and it was agreed that I was to have the first. I was still at Decatur,

Alabama, on actual duty of Captain and A.Q.M.
When about to join my regiment and [be] put on
duty by General Sheridan to fill a week's duty in place
of an absent lieutenant-colonel, word came from General Stanley's headquarters that the appointment had
been made in Washington."

But he was too late, by a week, in deciding to apply:
by the time the appointment came, the War was over,
and instead of taking on new officers the Army was
mustering out old ones by the hundred. His new
honor was a barren one, if indeed it had any real
existence; for the "word" that he mentions above
seems to have been merely an oral message from a staff
officer, and it has no discoverable documentary confirmation. His papers contain the three commissions
issued to him by the State of Wisconsin, but nothing
further. He himself in later years always denied that
he had the right to call himself more than first
lieutenant.

But when he was mustered out, on December 23,
1865, it was not to return to Janesville, and the bookstore, and his mother. Nor does he seem to have
looked at once for regular employment elsewhere; he
is not known to have been at work again for more
than a year. And the intervening year—1866—is one
that he often speaks of hoping to bury among "those
things which I have tried to forget." It is one of the
"secret years" of his life, various periods about which
we know nothing from his own records, and for whose
events we must search elsewhere. It was spent in Mt.

Vernon, Ohio; and his letters contain only one reference to his year there. It was a protest against the statement—in a newspaper—that he had sung in the choir of Father Mulhane's Catholic church in Mt. Vernon. "Now I am not a singer, and never was," he writes. "I only sat in the choir loft, in company with the young lady who played the organ and who had charge of the musical affairs of that church for many years." In the same letter he says, "A friend in California knows something of my life, and of the life-changing events at Mt. Vernon, Ohio, in 1866." Those "life-changing events" can now be described, though to tell their full tale will carry us somewhat ahead of our story.

Doubtless, the conscientious biographer should ordinarily present all the relevant facts at his disposal; but it seems kinder, in describing Ira Dutton's unhappy marriage, to commit to silence the name of the woman he married. No good purpose would be served now by mentioning it. But the sorrow and disappointment that she brought him for fifteen years are a real part of his life and probably had a substantial influence on his after-career.

The date when the two first met seems to have been about a year before the War ended, and the place was a town not far from Decatur, where Dutton had gone with several of his fellow-officers to some social affair at the house of one of the well-known Union families of the neighborhood. The young woman was an Ohioan, visiting Tennessee friends with her mother

THE PRESENT CHURCH AT KALAWAO

LEPER BOYS AT THE COTTAGE

and sister. And when she and Ira met they fell in love at once. She was evidently rather beautiful, with a good figure, the sort of attractive girl that young Ira had seen only too little of during his years of camp life; and she looked like his mother: a fact a psychologist would note. He, on his side, was a handsome and confident young officer, and it is easy to understand his attraction for her. By the time she went back to Ohio, they were engaged.

For a time, though he saw her frequently, he said nothing to his men friends about the affair. When, however, he did speak of his engagement, he was to hear some frank and unpalatable facts about the young woman. Others knew her better than he did, and presently, when it appeared that he was in earnest, and intended to be married as soon as he should be mustered out, they told him what they knew of the girl's character and previous history: she was not to be trusted—she was not truthful—she was easy-going sexually—and if he married her he would be asking for trouble. To all of this his answer was that "if she does have the faults you mention, I will make her better." That this confidence in the reforming power of matrimony is common does not make it any less tragic in the individual instance.

His friends were persistent. Up until the time that they started back to Wisconsin they tried to dissuade him. But Ira Dutton was never one—then or later—to let others settle his problems for him; and in this project he became only the firmer, sure that such "passing faults" could soon be "smoothed out." And in Mt. Vernon, nine days after he was mustered out, he married the girl. He seems to have had no regular work, and very little money. Indeed, before coming north he had borrowed from his friends, and later was to borrow more. The number of soldiers returning home made it hard, of course, to find employment; and for a time the young people lived with her family. He was deeply in love, but none the less began almost at once to discover in his wife some of the faults of which he had been warned. She sought admiration, she revealed a tendency to extravagance. Though her husband was poor and had no work, she ran up bills—bills that he had to borrow money to pay. Presently—toward the end of 1866—he found out that she had been unfaithful to him. He forgave her. The offense was repeated, not once but several times. We have no exact knowledge of what happened then between them, but in January, 1867, we find him in Memphis, looking for work. When he did get a position and at last was able to begin paying off his loans, his wife proceeded to run up more bills, so that for a third time he was forced to borrow from friends. When this story reaches the subject of Dutton's efforts to pay off this indebtedness, the reader is to bear in mind that it sprang not from his extravagance but from his wife's. Whether or not she spent the whole of 1867 in Mt. Vernon we have no means of knowing; but it is certain that at the end of that year she went to New York City with another man.

Ira Dutton gives no hint about what he felt when this news reached him from his friends. We know that he took no action for fourteen years—that it was not until May, 1881, that he sued for divorce. It is tempting to seek some connection between this desertion and what he was to call the sinfulness of that period—those "wild oats" which we shall discuss later and find not to have been so wild, after all. It needs no great imagination to conceive the effect on him of the shattering of his hopes for a happy marriage, of the conviction that his friends had been right in warning him. But whatever the effect, it did not discourage him from doing his best to induce her to return to him. He sent her money in New York, he wrote again and again begging her to leave the other man and come back to him; he seems to have been ready to forgive her—which in itself is both unusual and creditable. His letters brought no response, though the bills she had contracted turned up faithfully.

His divorce petition is brief, charging merely that after the marriage his wife had been guilty of adultery with "sundry persons on divers occasions." There was no defense; his wife was not even represented by a lawyer. The court agreed that the facts alleged had been proven; the divorce was granted, and costs were paid by Dutton.

There had been many unfounded stories circulated, both at the time and since, about this marriage. One, for instance, speaks of a child, who died. There was no child. The wife died shortly after the divorce, but there is no evidence suggesting that the divorce had anything to do with her death; indeed, she appears to have forgotten Ira Dutton completely long before that. The effect that the divorce was to have on him, on the other hand, played a large part in his future life. But before describing it we must return to his experiences from 1867 onward.

On going to Memphis early in January, 1867, he met Colonel A. W. Wills, who had been a brother-officer in the Army of the Cumberland and a close friend. At the instance of General George H. Thomas, on whose staff Wills had served, he had been assigned to the duty of locating and buying national cemetery lands in the Southwest, and he now engaged Dutton as one of his superintendents. Wills says, "I constructed the cemeteries at Corinth (Mississippi) and Pittsburg Landing (Tennessee), and it was then that Dutton was engaged in caring for the bodies of the heroic dead of the battlefields."

This task of Dutton's, which was to last for a year, was not a pleasant one. In thousands of unmarked and hidden graves lay scattered the unidentified dead of the Union armies. When he signed up once more under the United States Government as quartermaster's agent, he was to help in collecting these bodies and placing them in the newly established national cemeteries. With his men he must search every place where there had been fighting—not only the actual battlefields but the sites of smaller skirmishes, lonely forests and winding lanes where pickets had been surprised by raiders; for in all such places there were bodies hastily buried. Every body had to be taken from the ground, searched, and if possible identified; any property found on it must be sent to the dead soldier's family. Forty years afterward Dutton was to describe the work thus:

"Even before the close of the War a beginning was made in formulating plans for the national cemeteries and for the gathering of the dead. Soon after, the surrender work was begun, the organization being in groups conforming somewhat to the former lines of military divisions. Some of the dead, when in good condition, remained at rest in public cemeteries. Some, when in number not great enough to establish a new cemetery, were placed in the nearest burying-grounds attached to military posts—usually the old established posts. The greater number of the Federal dead left on battlefields, in fact in all the regions fought over, were gathered and placed in the newly formed national cemeteries located in the Southern States.

"Speaking offhand, the total Federal dead, say 360,-000, now rest in some 83 or 84 places; in the special manner described above, in say 43 or 44 places, in rather small numbers; one of 25, quite a number of a few hundred each, a few of one, two, or three thousand. The great majority being in the 40 newly constructed cemeteries, from a few thousands up to the larger ones such as Arlington (nearly 17,000), Nashville and Vicksburg (nearly the same), and Memphis (about 14,000). I speak from memory, but am close.

"As to gathering the dead for these, the territory

was divided.  A capable officer was assigned to this part, first duty being to locate the cemeteries, purchase the ground, etc.  Our Colonel Wills of General Thomas's staff did the first work over the Department of the Cumberland, and constructed the Corinth and Pittsburg Landing cemeteries, with oversight of Vicksburg.  I served with him for almost two years, looking after the gathering of the dead.  Was later for a long while at Chalmette, Louisiana.

"Few people have any idea of these almost sacred duties.  The work of locating the cemeteries was difficult; in some places hard engineering work had to be done to make the site usable.  So far as I can judge, cemeteries, when completed and turned over to the appointed keepers—usually ex-soldiers—were found satisfactory and have required little work save to be kept in order.

"The gathering of the bodies was delicate work. They were greatly scattered.  It was very important to locate all the trenches, groups, and scattered graves. The landmarks placed at some of the graves, even the trench graves themselves, were rapidly losing all signs by which they could be identified.  It was important that all the bodies be found at once and a record made so that they could not be lost.  This could not be done along with other work and required one, two, and even three years in some places.  So we sent surveying parties out at once in every dirction, certain territory allotted to each, to find every burial place and grave, and then to mark them on good maps; to do everything that common sense would dictate and to make each location sure.  Each location was numbered, and the maps were turned over to the one in charge of the disinterring party.

"We went out with tents and full camp outfits. Thus it happened that my 'tent life' lasted for somewhat more than six years. The disinterring parties had to go slower than the surveying parties, for we carried coffins and a large number of tools. Many of the bodies in coffins had to be hauled distances for shipment to the cemetery. Then there must always be a careful guard. None of the bodies could be removed from the grave where found until the one in charge had recorded everything, for which there was a complete set of blanks and record books. So far as possible I made it a rule to be present at the disinterment of every body. This required rapid going about and rapid writing. I thus made a record of about 6,000 bodies.

"Found many souvenirs on bodies. Many relatives and friends have been greatly comforted by seeing and being allowed to keep various articles found with the bodies of their dead, found in the clothing or placed by the body when buried. All these items I carefully collected and sent in separately. All marks upon boards or on any sort of material found at the graves were written in full in the records. Some of them were very curious and interesting; the comrades of many of the dead used odd things to mark the graves—devices none of us would think of. They expected, of course, to make a better record later, but the movements of troops prevented this in many cases.

"There were many interesting problems in the work, some relating to science and curious action by water or minerals; in some cases bodies were like stone. I found a large number of these at and around Iuka, Mississippi, a region having a good number of mineral springs, and the doctors came for miles around to see these bodies; sometimes [there was] an extensive growth of hair after death."

The long reminiscence of which this is a part contained also a passage that reveals his characteristic consideration for all those with whom he had to deal, even indirectly:

"While going over the country I made a private memorandum of the Confederate dead I came upon in out-of-the-way places. This I turned over to some public-spirited men of the South when I left that region. I have lately been trying to remember who they were, as I note an effort being made at this time to locate these graves. There were hundreds of items and records; I thought it best to make them for I could not think of these men lying unknown and forgotten."

In the letter that Brother Joseph had printed in 1928 and sent out from Molokai to nearly five hundred friends throughout the world, he gives the date January 31, 1868, as that on which he ended this work; though elsewhere he says that he was "engaged in cemeterial work for almost two years." But it was on this date that Colonel Wills resigned as head of the department under which Dutton was working, and it is probable that the latter ended his duties simultaneously. The reader must bear in mind, in connection

with various such discrepancies in this chronicle, that
many facts found in Dutton's letters were set down
when he was an old man, with an old man's hazy and
sometimes confused memory; and that when these are
contradicted by independent testimony—such as that
of his friend Miss Simmons—all that has been possible
is to present both versions.  A case in point is the degree and duration of his habit of drinking, which
seems to have set in shortly after the end of the "cemeterial work."

His next employment was as superintendent of a
United States Registered distillery in Alabama.  This,
again, we know through others rather than through
his own writings.  One of his family reports that he
was so employed from early in 1868 to the end of 1870,
though a search of the Internal Revenue Service lists
gives no evidence that he was at any of the five distil-
leries then operating in Alabama.  He must have been
employed in some private plant, perhaps as superintendent.  We do not know; nor do we know why he
gave up this work toward the end of 1870 and became
a clerk in a railroad office.  All that we may be sure of
is that these years belong to the secret life of which he
was so ashamed that he would not speak of them.

One day he dropped into the Memphis office of the
Louisville & Nashville Railroad looking for a position.
He seems to have been without money; what pay he
got at the distillery was evidently all gone.  The clerkship given him was to constitute his first really sub-
ordinate position—up to this time he had always been

in charge of other men. Now he was to start at the bottom, as freight check clerk in the yards and warehouses. After some years he was promoted to the office, where he became chief clerk at (as he says) "one side of the freight agent's big double desk. Attended to the overs, shorts, and damages, besides making up the office payroll and replacing agents who were sick along the line. It looked very much as if I had become a fixture in the railroad office."

Of his Memphis life Dutton always wrote freely. It seems to have been a not unhappy period altogether. For a time he roomed at the old Navy Yard quarters, but when he became chief clerk the agent, a Horace Smith, asked him to live at his house. "They had a roomy place, with stables and horses, and we drove in fine style to the office every morning. This was about 1875." Presently he made friends among the "best people" of the city—evidence of something winning in his nature, considering that he was a Northerner who had fought in the Union Army, and that these were the days of the hated carpet-bagger. Dutton was invited to their homes and made a personal friend. And the associations of these years were not to die out; as late as 1929 Dutton was writing to the grandchildren of his Memphis friends, and all his life he took a Memphis daily paper.

His letters from Molokai are full of names of persons whom he met in this way. He knew Jefferson Davis's family and dined several times with them in the period between the collapse of the Confederacy

and the date when they moved to Beauvoir.   He mentions other well-known names in Southern society—
Mason, Semmes, Stoddart, Carruthers; all these families were his friends.   There are references to dinners
and dances, parties, drives into the country.   He had
his own saddle-horse.   Altogether, his outer life was
pleasant.   Then his occupation was to change once
more.

"I felt that the rest of my life would be in railroad-
ing.   I had a good position and many friends, and
there were no doubt promotions ahead.   At the close
of 1875 I had been with the railroad five years.   In
November I was offered an appointment with the War
Department.   About a year before this I had received
a hint that such a thing might happen, and I had indicated that if it did I would accept such a duty; but
hearing nothing, concluded that it was not to be.
Thus, when it came it found me somewhat perplexed.
I talked it over with Mr. Smith, and it was agreed that
I should take three days to study the matter.   Service
with Uncle Sam carried the day.   This service lasted
eight years, in Ohio, Tennessee, and Kentucky; Memphis much of the time.   My headquarters were in
Memphis, and my second appointment was by Robert
Lincoln, Secretary of War."

He was appointed investigating agent for the War
Department, adjusting claims in the three States mentioned, the greater part of his work being concerned
with the claims of persons who had remained loyal to
the Union during the War, many of whom had lost all

they had either through the havoc of warfare or by the deliberate acts of their Southern neighbors. The charge has been made that he spent too much time and attention on getting pensions for Union soldiers. The records do not bear out the charge. This was a part of his duty, but a very minor part. Chiefly he was busy settling citizens' claims against the Government for food and horses requisitioned for Union troops. There were small claims and large; some persons pressed for higher damages than the facts warranted, and there were plenty of folk zealous to see that no neighbor should be overpaid. Altogether it was a delicate task, requiring tact and patience, and above all the ability to conciliate aggrieved cupidity. There is a significant comment from one lawyer who had to present many claims before Ira Dutton. Judge Stout of Clarksville, who is still living, says, "Of all the different men the Government sent here, I thought he was the fairest and most impartial." Dutton spent some time in this Tennessee town in 1881, and was to be there briefly once more in his life, when he was on his way to Molokai. Clarksville recalls him as a handsome and rather dashing person whose graciousness and gayety won the hearts of the local belles.

He may have been all that, outwardly; the record of his inner life during these years is streaked darkly with uncertainty and remorse. The story, to be complete, must cover the "sinfulness" of which he spoke so often afterward. Yet as we weigh the details that he himself furnishes, and other persons' reports, we cannot but conclude that he exaggerated both the character and the amount of his wrongdoing.  It has been mentioned that at several times he was heavily in debt, and undoubtedly the need of paying off his loans worried him during many years.  But an allegation that has sometimes appeared in print, to the effect that these debts sprang from his manner of living—his drinking and gambling—is quite untrue; the fact being that he went into debt to meet the bills contracted by his wife both while they lived together and afterward.  And from 1880 to the end of 1883 he was saving carefully from his salary and gradually paying off his loans with interest, until eventually he had repaid all his creditors but two.

"The two were good friends of mine; one had been in my service during the War, the other I knew in Tennessee.  When I tried to pay them I could not discover where they had gone.  For years I thought about them, trying to find where they were, in order to have my slate clean; but they died, and I had failed to repay what was needed to complete the record.  It was my own neglect and carelessness, and I am remembering it now and ask God to forgive me.  I did pay up as well as I then knew, but failed to pay these two souls, whom I always pray for."

Not all of the persons to whom he owed money would accept repayment.  In several cases the money was returned with the message that "he owed nothing."  He mentions one friend, a former army officer, whose protest he overrode and succeeded in paying the

$179 due.

None of these debts seem to have sprung from gambling, though there is an occasional reference to card-playing, losses and winnings alternating. But this cannot be judged too severely, considering the prevalent customs in the Southwest fifty years ago. It would indeed have been remarkable if he had not gambled. Once or twice, too, he went to a horse-race, and like everybody else put his money on the horse that came in last. Nothing so far, evidently, sounds like "wild oats" of the serious character implied by his later life-long penitence. What may have been more serious was his drinking.

The relative of whom he said that "she knows more about me than I do myself"—Miss Simmons—believes that the drinking began while he was in the Alabama distillery. But his own statement is to a different effect:

"At the close of the War I was, as to general conduct, about as before, no better, no worse. Just what brought on the difference I must not state here—never have. [We may conclude that he was referring to his marriage.] Some day, perhaps, someone will find the record, and if they do it will be well. Anyway, I allowed the demon of drink to get me into its clutches. The sort of associations that follow hard drinking became part of my life, and I was very foolish. It was truly a dual life that I lived. At night there would be one sort of associations, and then by day a care for sobriety and respectable company. In all the time, I had good, responsible employment. But there were comrades who knew of the nights and my pretty constant employment with John Barleycorn. They sought to draw me away from the evil part of life; especially did the officials and employees of the L. & N. Railroad. Long had my conduct pained them.

"Cannot recall any particular incident that caused me to change my life; think it was shame for acting so among capable, sober, well-balanced men, and feeling that having even a little authority I should have a clear head, and feeling so mean after my sober Civil War record. Anyway, I determined to kick John Barleycorn out of my house, and so it was. As soon as this was noticed, the agent, Horace F. Smith, invited me to take up my abode with him, and I did so."

Another paper of Dutton's mentions his taking the pledge.

"Perhaps I never injured anyone but myself; but I was subject to various follies that attend the use of strong drink, a habit acquired in this reckless period. In getting the upper hand of John Barleycorn, and out of his clutches, I recall the date—July 4, 1876—because of making on that day a voluntary, private vow: my declaration of independence. (I leave the capital letters for the Declaration of 1776.) A declaration against John B. Since that, I have kept the vow, being free of intoxicants and—so far as I can judge now—of all the attendant folly.

"But how about the mischief I had done myself, and the regrets I had caused among many very dear friends, who still remain friends and who rejoiced over the

reform? You may say, 'All was well then.' Ah, but
how about Almighty God and the wicked capers I cut?
We will see about that later. But it was sorrow for
those days, and the idea of doing penance, that led me
out of the world."

All this is pretty vague, of course—perhaps inten-
tionally so. In any case it has led to many attempts to
read between the lines, and to read sensationally. A
few months before Dutton's death a magazine article
stated that at one time he drank so heavily that he was
"down and out and in the gutter." This story goes on
to say that a kindly priest found him, took him to the
rectory, and befriended him; and that because of this
service he turned over a new leaf, sobered up, and a
few months later—as a result of the priest's instruction
—went into the Church. This is but one more story
with no foundation in truth. Dutton himself gives us
the date of the pledge, and we know that his entrance
into the Church was not decided on until eight years
after that.

And though this vagueness characterizes all his statements about his years of drinking, they are repeated so
many times, and with such earnestness, that we cannot
but believe the general fact. Yet we need not go so far
as to think of him as ever having been a helpless victim of alcohol; he may have taken too much fairly
frequently during the seven years, but his character as
we know it suggests that he could have stopped at any
moment when he wanted to stop; as indeed he did,
once and for all, in 1876. "From the time I took the

LOOKING SEAWARD FROM THE BALDWIN HOME

pledge I never used intoxicants—never felt any desire
to use them after I stopped."

Here again, in judging him, we must remember
that drinking was not, fifty years ago in the South, considered as an anti-social act; rather quite the contrary.
But it seems that in his case abstinence, when once re-
solved on, was approved by the friends closest to him,
and led to his being offered a home with his chief.

Before leaving the subject of the pledge, we may
note yet another discrepancy in dates. The date July
4, 1876, appears in a memorandum that Dutton gave
to Albert Taylor, librarian of Hawaiian archives, a
five-page account of his life containing the phrase, "I
recall the date July 4, 1876, because of making my
voluntary vow of independence." Then—"I note now
by my record that in November, 1875, more than half
a year before the 'declaration,' I had been appointed
investigating agent for the War Department." But in
a long letter to Frank Waterbury of Des Moines he
tells the story differently, fixing the date of the pledge
as 1875. "This was about 1875, early in that year,
probably, having been with the railroad a little more
than five years. Then, in the fall of 1875, offered employment with the Government." It is possible to
reconcile these two statements by supposing that in
1875 he decided to reduce or cut off altogether his
consumption of liquor; and then in 1876 took the
pledge to seal his decision.

It was soon after this that, while traveling about
from town to town as claim agent, Ira Dutton began to

do what must be considered—for him—a rather curious thing, even when we bear in mind the remorse that was stirring in his soul already, and his growing tendency to self-condemnation. Perhaps the explanation that would occur most readily to the devout is the correct one: that God was "working His purposes out." Without talking about it to his friends he began to visit churches of various denominations, and to study and compare their beliefs. He had, before this, left the Baptist church of his boyhood and in Memphis had entered the Protestant Episcopal church. Presently, however, he was not to be seen at its services, and new words crept into his vocabulary: he began to talk of his "wild years" and his "sinful capers"; he spoke of "penance" often. Then he sold his saddlehorse, and joined in fewer of the good times of his Clarksville friends. He grew grave and thoughtful, this young man who had always been spoken of as laughing and pleasure-loving. His reading was no longer novels; he was studying the Catholic catechism.

Then in 1881 came his divorce, closing that unhappy chapter of his life. And not very long afterward another chapter was to open. He decided to enter the Catholic Church. Let him tell of it in his own words:

"In 1882, while yet working for the Government, I had decided upon a life of penance for the rest of my years. I decided that the penitential system of the Catholic Church was best suited for my condition. After a daily study of the catechism for a month at St.

Peter's Church, Memphis, I was received into the Church on my fortieth birthday, April 27, 1883."

This was the occasion on which he changed his name.

"I always had a special respect for the name of Saint Joseph. My name, Ira, was not a Christian name, though it appears in the Old Testament. So I asked for, and received, conditional baptism in the name of Saint Joseph, because of several years' devotion to Saint Joseph, who led me straight into the arms of the historic Church to enjoy its great penitential system. For I had committed sin. My United States service was to end at the close of the year 1883, and I had to continue the use of my name Ira B. Dutton in all the official work. But at the close of 1883 I was disposed to be a new person, Joseph Dutton, a servant of Our Lord; so, reverently laying aside the 'Ira B.,' I was Joseph, stepping out to a new life."

Of the human agency chiefly responsible for Dutton's conversion several varying stories are told. The most familiar of these—to the effect that he was converted by a hotel housekeeper in Clarksville—is to be doubted, though it is the one that has been widely printed, and even broadcast on the air. For it purports to be his own account of the matter, and yet we find no mention of it in any of his letters. It runs thus: a Mrs. Julia Sullivan, a kindly and devout Irish widow, intent on the comfort of the residents in the hotel, was given to leaving Catholic books and tracts in their rooms; and when she noticed that these were being read by Dutton, she brought him more and more—they ended by persuading him of the unique merits of the Church.  We confess to doubting the story, for which there is no confirmation in our documents; yet we must own that for the version that we incline to there is just as little confirmatory evidence. We present it, however, for what it is worth.

Among Dutton's closest friends in Memphis were the Semmes family.  Mrs. Benedict J. Semmes had been an Easterner, and in earlier years had known Washington Irving, Edgar Allan Poe, and other distinguished men.  Her house in Memphis constituted the city's cultural center; and here Dutton spent many hours.  The statement is significant, for the Semmeses were strongly Southern in their sympathies.  Mrs. Semmes's husband had been an officer in the Confederate Army; his cousin had commanded the *Alabama*. But the trust and affection with which he was received in the Semmes house were sincere, and the friendship was to last for many years—indeed until Mrs. Semmes died at the age of ninety-six.  It was a devout Catholic home, and we have Ira Dutton's own statement that while he was considering entering the Church he brought all his difficulties to Mrs. Semmes for discussion.  He told her, he says, "all my past life, and what I had in mind.  For a while she tried to dissuade me from the step I thought of taking, saying that she doubted whether my disposition was fitted for it."  No coercion here, obviously.  The Catholic friend who was closest to him, who might have been expected to use every means to bring him into her Church, judicially weighed the matter instead, sought to determine whether he would be doing the right thing to enter it, even "tried to dissuade him." But we may be sure that no one rejoiced more than she when his decision was made; and it was she whom he chose as his godmother when he was ready for the sacrament of baptism.

The priest who prepared him was a well-known Dominican of Memphis, the Rev. Father Joseph Kelly, who during the four epidemics of yellow fever that visited the city from 1867 onward had proved himself a saint and a hero. He had nursed the sick and visited the dying without distinction of faith. It is likely that Ira Dutton met him frequently at the Semmes house, so that it may have been a friend to whom the postulant went for instruction and help.

His letters reveal something of what was going on in his mind at this time. "I had determined to spend the remainder of my life in penance for past wrongs, to find some work without pay where I could be helpful and do my best for all." Where this decision might lead him he did not yet know. "To try my courage and stability, I was disposed to study several forms of this new manner of life, not making formal vows anywhere, at least for the present."

And at the end of 1883 the Ira Dutton who was so familiar a figure in Memphis society dropped out of sight. His disappearance was talked of for some days, and the rumor went around that he had retired from the world, that he had become a monk. To a certain extent the rumor was true. He was not to become a monk, or a priest; he never took vows, and so was not technically entitled to the "Brother" which was later prefixed to his name. But it was true that the world that had known Ira Dutton was to know him no more. In his place, after a year or two, there was to appear Brother Joseph Dutton, missionary to the lepers.

# CHAPTER X

## THE PENITENT

JOSEPH DUTTON knocked at the door of the Trappist monastery at Gethsemane, Kentucky. Beyond, he might find peace. What he had been was bookstore clerk, soldier, distillery superintendent, railroad freight agent, Government investigator of claims. What at this moment he was hoping to become we do not know. Probably he did not himself know. But he had been brought to realize that his life was not satisfactory, not happy—not right; and here perhaps he could find readjustment.

This monastery was one of several religious houses that he had visited in the course of his Government travels, and after he entered the Catholic Church he recalled how much he had been impressed by what he had seen of the "Abbey of Our Lady of Gethsemani." And here his memories drew him now, to stay for twenty months among the Trappist monks.

That the Trappist order, with its rule of perpetual silence, should ever have become acclimated in the United States is a strange phenomenon. But in Ira Dutton's day the Order had one house in this country, and by now there are three more: one in Rhode Island, another in Oregon, and the well-known monastery founded by priests from an abbey in Ireland, and situated near Dubuque, Iowa. He had already learned the history of Gethsemani, and no doubt had been told something also of the history of the order.

Its founder was Armand-Jean le Bouthillier de Rancé, godson of Cardinal Richelieu, who toward the end of the seventeenth century bade farewell to the glittering court of which he had been a part and, turning his back on the past, retired to the ancient abbey of La Trappe in Normandy, where he undertook the task of reforming the relaxed Benedictines. This abbey had been favored with gifts from many Popes, but it was a gloomy place, hidden in a deep, fog-swept valley and surrounded by thick woods. And when de Rancé reached it he found it falling into utter ruin, its walls crumbling, its inmates a few half-starved priests. Here he spent the rest of his long life; and at his death the abbey was once again a flourishing institution, filled with men who, defeated by life or stricken by conscience, had come to this retreat to end their days in penance and silence.

The French Revolution drove the Trappist monks out of their own country to become wanderers in other lands, and their abbey was converted into a foundry for the making of cannon. It was in 1804 that the first group came to this country—a small band who established themselves in Pennsylvania. But being dissatisfied there for some reason, they moved on after a few months toward the still wild and little-known country of Kentucky. This was a natural move, for

although Maryland is the leading Catholic center of
the seaboard, Kentucky was the inland territory to be
settled earliest by the French missionaries who traveled along the Wabash and the Mississippi.  After the
French Revolution priests from France who had been
exiled found in Kentucky a refuge among fellow-
countrymen and coreligionists, and it was here that
the first episcopal see of their Church was founded in
the West.

The monks who had come from Pennsylvania settled first only a few miles from the future site of the
Abbey of Gethsemani.  But their superior was a restless man, and he wanted, besides, to convert the Indian
children in Missouri; so they moved on again, and
then once more, into Illinois.  In the year 1813—when
the French Revolution was long past and the religious
orders were again permitted in France—the surviving
Trappists of this original group were recalled home.

The present monastery of Gethsemani owes its
origin to the abbey of Melleray in France.  The abbot
had intended to found a house on the island of Mar-
tinique, and got permission to do so from Louis
Philippe, King of the French, on whose estate there
the house was to be built.  But when he lost his throne
in 1848 the order was obliged to relinquish the Mar-
tinique plan, and decided to found a house in the
United States instead.  The two Brothers who were
sent over to find a site chose a place in Kentucky near
where the original group had once settled.  And in the
autumn a company of forty-eight religious sailed for

New Orleans.  They took boat up the river as far as Louisville, and walked sixty miles over country roads to reach the present site of Gethsemani.  Here they built the first abbey in the United States.

At the time that Joseph Dutton came knocking at its door, the abbey occupied an immense tract of rich farm land—nearly 1700 acres—with woods that furnished lumber for its sawmill.  When the Brothers received him they told him the character and extent of the obligations he must assume if he would live among them, and they warned him that many found the rules too strict, or during the probation period realized their unfitness for monastic life.  "Though I knew it was a severe discipline," he writes, "yet it seemed to be what I needed at the time."  It was to be some time before he reached the conclusion that he was better fitted for some other type of sacrificial life.

The monastic community at Gethsemani is divided into three classes.  The first are the choir brothers or choir religious, whose garb is the white cowl; they hold office and direct the chapel services; they have taken life vows of poverty, humility, silence, and obedience to the head of the order.  It is from this class that the higher positions in the abbey are filled, its members being of better birth or of superior intellectual ability.  Next below these come the lay brothers, men who have been taken into the order but have no voice in the management of its affairs, and are kept engaged at manual labor somewhat longer than are the choir religious.  The third group, the oblates and

novices, comprise persons merely associated with the
order and conforming to its rules during their residence, and those who are on probation and, because
they have not yet taken the oath, are free to leave when
they wish. The second and the third classes perform
the outdoor work on the farm, raising the grass and
grain, tilling the soil of the vast gardens and vineyards,
and operating the sawmills owned by the order.

When Joseph Dutton passed through the monastery
wall he became a member of the third group. He
never, either then or subsequently, took any vows.
"It seems well," he writes in one place, "to put this
matter on record. I am not under vows—have never
made any, not even in the twenty months when I lived
with the Trappists at Gethsemani. I did take with
Father Damien a yearly vow to serve the Catholic Mission at Molokai; but when the Brothers and Sisters
came, I stopped doing this. I am not and never have
been a Brother in the sense used by religious orders.
I am just a common, everyday layman. Various desig-
nations have been added by good friends in correspondence, such as Father, Brother, Venerable, etc.;
but I sign simply Joseph Dutton."

This should settle the old controversy over Joseph
Dutton's official title. He himself was indifferent in
the matter; in another of his letters he likens himself
to the man "who said he did not care what people
called him, if only they did not call him too late for
breakfast." And again, more seriously: "I still continue to sign just Joseph Dutton, but am often

tempted to add, 'brother to everybody.' "

But though he did not join the order he shared the life whose two chief rules are hard work and silence. To the Trappists idleness seems a snare of Satan, and manual labor an obligation. No entrant, whatever his station in life before, is excused from his share in the variety of tasks that make the abbey self-supporting and independent. But the work is done in silence, absolute and uninterrupted. There are only a few exceptions to the rule that the monks may not speak: when taking part in the offices of the Church, when confessing, and when they find a fellowman in need and must speak in order to help him.

It was a strictly ordered life that Joseph Dutton followed for twenty months. From his narrow bed, covered only with a sheet and a coarse, thin blanket, he rose at two in the morning to attend the first of the seven daily services in the chapel. This was over by dawn, and then came the simple breakfast, another service, and the work in the fields. Meat was never eaten. Each time that he passed the abbey cemetery he saw the open grave that had been prepared for the next Brother who should die. If there was a death in the abbey while he was there, he saw the body lying on a cross of ashes on the cold floor, and then carried out coffinless for burial. He might go beyond the walls only by permission; and we know that on one occasion he did so.

This actual incident was used by the Kentucky novelist James Lane Allen as the basis for his short

story, "The White Cowl," which gradually came to be
regarded by many readers as a true story about Brother
Joseph.   One of the abbey rules excludes women from
its confines, with two exceptions only—the wife of the
President of the United States and the wife of the Governor of Kentucky.   The incident that befell Joseph
Dutton had to do with a woman, but it happened outside of the walls, where he was busy cutting the grass
along the highway.

In "The White Cowl," a young monk who had
taken the vows of silence and chastity was working
near the abbey wall, and heard outside the voices of a
man and a woman.   The woman's voice aroused
thoughts which he felt impelled to bare in public confession.   Penance was imposed, and after it had been
fulfilled he was sent outside to teach in a little school.
Here the same woman crossed his path, and in the
school they met and talked and loved.   He asked the
abbot for release from his vows; refused, he went away
in the darkness, and was gone for many years.   The
woman he had loved died, and with her their child.
He crept back to the only refuge he knew, and was
taken into the abbey only when his desperate illness
was observed, and allowed to remain as a guest.
When, at the point of death, he was taken into the
death chamber, he saw the consecrated ashes sprinkled
on the floor and over them the scattered straw and
rough cloth that showed him that once more he was to
be admitted to their fellowship.   And when he died,
they threw over him the white cowl of the Trappist

monk.

This, however, is almost entirely fictitious. What had actually happened to Brother Joseph was merely that a passing horsewoman was thrown by her runaway horse and fell almost at his feet. He carried her to the schoolhouse nearby and left her in charge of the teacher. Allen heard this on a visit to the abbey and on it built his plot. When Joseph Dutton read the story, years later, he was much disturbed to be told that in the general belief it contained the reason for his having left the abbey.

The real reason why he left is very simple. It is not —as has sometimes been stated—that the Brothers doubted his sincerity or his fitness. If this were true they would hardly have remained his lifelong friends. But the realization growing in his mind during those months was that theirs was a life of contemplation, and what he wanted was a life of action. And as he went forth to find it he was accompanied by the prayers and good wishes of the monks. The discipline he had learned was not to be wasted, a stern discipline of flesh and spirit that was to make him stronger for the work that lay ahead.

It was to St. Louis that he first went, to visit other monastic establishments. There he met a friend, a Redemptorist Father, whose order had a house in New Orleans that Dutton already knew. When the priest went south Joseph Dutton was with him, and in the library of the Redemptorist house he first heard of Father Damien's work at Molokai.

"It was a new subject and attracted me wonderfully. After weighing it for a while I became convinced that it would suit my wants—for labor, for a penitential life, and for seclusion as well as complete separation from scenes of all past experiences. It seems a mere accident that I ever heard of this place, and it might never have happened again. In fact, the place was hardly known at all at that date—did not really become famous until about three years later when the death of Father Damien made it so. Yet I was not thinking to hide, exactly; it was a good deal the idea of 'beginning again.' But the real motive was to do some good for my neighbor and at the same time make it my penitentiary in doing penance for my sins and errors. The only question was, could I get in there and be useful?"

There is more detail in a letter to Frank Waterbury:

"I was at St. Louis and there met a Redemptorist Father, a former Provincial, about to go to a conference of the Order in New Orleans. We had many talks together, and he kindly invited me to go with him. They had churches there—German, French, and American. So when he invited me to go with him and visit the convent at New Orleans I accepted. I had been on duty there at the close of the Civil War, and liked the idea. It was there in the convent, in the reading-room, that I saw for the first time a mention of Father Damien—a brief item in an old-time Catholic paper about Molokai and the Father. I had never heard of him.

"Why this suddenly impressed me with the certainty that I had found my real vocation I have never tried to elucidate; but have acted as if there were need only to go ahead, leaving the whys and wherefores to any who like such problems. I learned later of Charles Warren Stoddard, professor at Notre Dame University, learned that he had been there, and at once decided to go and see him about getting to Molokai, and if it were sure I could find plenty of work. I went and, as I expected, was satisfied as to both, and set off at once."

It seems also that he read a small book that Stoddard had written about the leper settlement and Damien, a book that—even though its sale was not large—gave the public its first real information on the subject. Stoddard, it appears, assured Dutton of a welcome from Damien and told him how to reach the Hawaiian Islands. His mind made up now, he revisited Janesville for a short time. More than twenty years had passed since he had left his home. He was now the only living child of the family, and his father had died in 1879. His mother was thus left alone. What the two said when they met we have no means of knowing, or whether she demurred at his new plan to leave the country altogether. It is to be doubted: whatever her Ira had done was all right, and whatever the new Joseph planned to do must also be all right. As for his change of faith, that can only have made her happy, for she herself had entered the Catholic Church shortly before this—only a year, indeed, after her son had made his profession.

He spent some time settling up his private affairs, and seems to have had plenty of money, even after he

THE FLAG AT HALF-MAST ON MEMORIAL DAY

turned over to his mother the part of his father's estate that had been devised to him. How much he took with him when he went to Molokai cannot be stated; but it must have been a good deal, because in all his forty-four years on the Island he took no pay for his services and at the same time gave away a considerable amount—over $10,000 to charity during his residence there, and during the World War he put $1000 into Liberty Bonds. A few other visits to friends, and he would be ready to set out for Molokai.

He spent some time in Memphis, and for some reason that we cannot quite understand thought it obligatory upon him to go to Clarksville once more, in order to hunt up the young women he had known there and to apologize to them for not having told them before that he was married. Conscience, probably, a still somewhat exaggerated estimate of past derelictions. Then—

"I started from Memphis for San Francisco. Though I had ample means along, [I] came on an immigrant ticket, and from San Francisco on a sailing vessel—the cheapest way, carrying out the idea of making it a sort of pilgrimage."

He had now assumed the garb he was to wear for the rest of his life: a suit of cheap blue denim. The comforts and luxuries of the world he had once known were set aside finally. The story, however, that he left America secretly and in poverty—that he took the small sailing vessel at San Francisco because he could

not afford better—is evidently quite untrue; he himself
says that the decision was part of his penance.  As for
secrecy, he had told his friends where he was going
and what he expected to do.

Other equally apocryphal stories are told of his
procedure on arriving at Honolulu.  What he did
there was quite simple: as soon as he stepped off the
boat he presented himself to Bishop Hermann, showed
the letters he had brought from Notre Dame, and
asked to go to Molokai without pay.  What references—
if any—he may have made to his past life on this occasion we cannot tell.  But to the bishop he was a God-
send.  The leper settlement always needed helpers,
but the Church in Hawaii had not been able to spare
men.  Here was an applicant for the work, who had
traveled thousands of miles at his own expense to ask
for it, a volunteer for the life that others shunned.

But the bishop himself could not give the necessary
permission.  The Board of Health must be consulted,
and the King as well.  When Brother Joseph met the
president of the Board of Health it was to discover
that they were fellow-Vermonters, and this may explain the speed with which the question was brought
before the legislature and the required permission
granted.  In Brother Joseph's own words:

"Arriving at Honolulu, I at once called on Bishop
Hermann.  He saw Mr. Gibson, premier and president of the Board of Health, who asked that I come to
see him at his home.  I called twice.  He was inter-

ested, at once gave me authority for my coming, took me over to see another 'old Varmounter,' E. R. Hendry, clerk of the Board of Health. The latter and Mr. Gibson were very busy with the legislature, then in session. The legislature had also just returned from a general visit to the settlement. Father Damien had been in Honolulu for a few weeks, making a first trial of the Japanese treatment for leprosy, as the disease had just appeared on him. He came back with the legislature, had been trying the Japanese treatment at the branch hospital, then returned to Molokai. They gave the permission I desired.

"Mr. Gibson sent out Mr. Hendry to buy what they thought I would need. A lady at the Gibson home advised me as to cooking and the care I should take of myself, for matters were in rather a primitive form at the settlement and so continued for some years. Mr. Gibson offered me pay, but that did not at all fit in with my ideas. Wanted to give myself entirely free, and was so gladly accepted. A sort of sentiment, this might be regarded as, but there was nothing bad about it, and I feel the same way yet. Am glad to say the Board of Health and my good friends have always honored this feeling.

"The steamer was not making the trip to Molokai that week, but Mr. Gibson arranged to have it come and call for my passage; but I had already bought a ticket ahead of him. The steamer left me at Kalaupapa on July 29, 1886, nearly three years before Father Damien died. And I have never left the grounds of the leper settlement—in fact, have not been away from the Baldwin Home for years."

It is interesting to speculate on what Brother Joseph's thoughts must have been as the steamer bore him south toward Molokai, and presently the tall cliffs behind the leper colony showed themselves above the horizon.   Forty-three years of one kind of life lay behind him; forty-four years of a new kind were awaiting him under those cliffs.   We are told that two intentions were firmly fixed: "to get along with everybody by attending to my own affairs, and to consider myself just a servant to my fellowmen."

# CHAPTER XI

On a clear, bright morning of July, in 1886, two men met on the sandy beach of Molokai. The waters of the Pacific danced in the sunshine, and the high cliffs in the distance were radiant. Not far away was the cluster of green huts marking the non-leper community of Kalaupapa. The tall man whom the steamer had just landed was smiling gravely as he waited in silence for his welcome. The other was a pathetic, almost forbidding, figure, his skin burnt black by the tropic sun, ears grotesquely enlarged by the disease that was already upon him, his queer dress fitting him awkwardly. It was a pregnant encounter, for it was to open three years of happy and constructive collaboration between Joseph Dutton and Father Damien.

Presumably Damien had no idea who this stranger was, or why he had come. Dutton had spent only a few days in Honolulu, and after Damien had left for the settlement. In those days no radio sent its messages from one Island to another, and there is no evidence to suggest that Damien had been forewarned. His coming down to meet the boat that day was merely a part of his old habit of being on hand to greet any new lepers who might be landed or officials coming for inspection.   Dutton has described the first interview.

"Forty years ago this morning I landed at Kalaupapa.   Father Damien was there waiting, with his
buggy—low, wide, and rattling—and a steady old horse.
I introduced myself as coming with King Kalakaua's
permission.   (It was before the Islands became a part
of our country.)   We climbed into the buggy and were
off to Kalawao.   The autos that whiz everywhere nowadays were unknown then.   Father Damien's old
buggy would be a curio now.

"Kalaupapa was a town of non-lepers then, and
Father Damien had a church there, while he lived by
the one at Kalawao, the leper settlement, where he
had been for about thirteen years.   He was now a
leper in the advanced stage; he died nearly three years
later.   I was happy as we drove over that morning.
The Father talked eagerly, telling how he had wanted
Brothers here, but the mission had none to spare yet.
So he called me Brother, as I had come to stay, and
gave me at once the care of two churches.   He was full
of plans that morning, talking of what he wished for
his lepers, the dreams he had always had."

Dutton lunched that day with Dr. Arthur A. Mouritz, who has already been mentioned as the physician
of the leper colony, and who describes the new worker
thus:

"Brother Dutton took lunch with me, and I scanned
him carefully. . . . It was a hot dusty trip, yet Dutton
showed no fatigue nor travel-stained clothes.   He wore
a blue denim suit, which fitted his tall, well-knit, slim,

muscular figure.  He stood about five feet seven inches tall, had dark brown hair and grayish blue eyes, a low voice, placid features, and a pleasant smile.  He was reserved and thoughtful, had nothing to say about his past life or the reason for his seeking seclusion and work at Molokai and turning his back forever on the world."

The resolutions with which Dutton had come have been quoted briefly.  Elsewhere he enlarges on his motives:

"I was firm in at least one resolve: to get along with everyone, to ask no special favors, not to make anyone the slightest difficulty that I could reasonably avoid, and to do what I could to help my neighbor in every way.  It has always been my hope never to falter in this, and [I] may add (what is also really part of the same) to carefully and fearlessly mind my own business, not mixing in the affairs of others.  This was the resolution in my heart when I came here.  In this, my twentieth year here, I may say that I am sure no one can stand 'forninst me' and cite any important failure of mine in these."

The newcomer's first few days were spent in Damien's house, a small cottage beside the church, its doors always left open so that the lepers might come and go as they chose.  On the first night they thronged the veranda and crowded to the windows, eager for a sight of the man who they had learned was come to share their lot.  Dutton presently moved to a house of his own, a few yards away, but for a year and a half longer he took all his meals with the priest.

Just what he was to do he did not yet know, though he had been assured at Notre Dame that there would be plenty of work, and of many different kinds. Conditions at the colony were immeasurably better than they had been when Father Damien came, but they were still far from what they were to become when Molokai was known as the finest leper colony in the world. Around him Brother Joseph saw the rude grass huts and shacks that were then the only dwellings for the lepers. The water-supply was still insufficient. There was a medical man on the Island, but the hospital was without the trained nurses so urgently needed. Yes, there was plenty of work for him to do, and he plunged in the day after his arrival. Henceforward, from daybreak until late at night, he was cleaning and dressing sores, attending to ulcers and other skin troubles. From Dr. Mouritz he learned the rudiments of surgery, and was trained in removing the dead bones from arms and legs, in dressing wounds, and in the various methods of applying bandages. All day long he went from hut to hut, until in the end (we are assured) he knew more about this sort of medical work than did the doctor himself. As soon as he was sufficiently expert he had all these duties turned over to him by Father Damien, who until then had been looking after them himself. Damien had done all these things independently of medical advice, and so

THE BALDWIN HOME FOR LEPERS, KALAWAO, MOLOKAI

A GROUP OF BOYS WITH THEIR DIRECTORS AT THE REAR OF THE BALDWIN HOME

from time to time had brought down on his head the severe criticism of visiting physicians. Dutton was more cautious and acted always under the doctor's supervision.

"When there was—or when there was not—a resident physician on the Island, he [Damien] kept a supply of drugs, which he prescribed for the many sick. A number of the natives would call on him instead of on a resident physician. His treatment of the sick continued until the summer of 1887, when he turned the drugs over to me. I kept them for use at the mission house under the direction of the physician. As for Damien's relations with the physician, it somewhat depended on who the physician was. Some were satisfied with his practising as he did; others—one in particular—opposed. And because of this opposition he discontinued it and gave me the drugs. Up to the summer of 1887 he dressed the lepers' sores, but after I came the task fell on me, as I wished."

But this medical work was only a part of the job, which grew and ramified as jobs have a way of doing when they fall into the hands of a willing and ingenious person. As long as Damien was alive, of course, Dutton was his assistant, to help him, to talk over new plans with him, to finish up the undone tasks that Damien started. For Damien was never orderly, never careful of details. His enthusiasm led him to begin things, but he was likely to leave off when they were half done and turn to something fresh. It was here that Dutton was useful: he could tie up the loose ends.   He has said that it was Damien's habit to

"drive ahead at what he thought was most important, until he thought something else was more important, when he would jump over into that.   Thus he always left a track of unfinished jobs, though a certain share would be completed.   It seemed sometimes that he tried to do more than one person could do or ever expect to finish."

A more significant point of contrast between the two was their respective attitudes toward the danger of infection.   We have seen how careless Damien was.   But it was characteristic of the orderly Dutton that his precautions were unremitting.   For example he always used scrubbing-brush and soap on all instruments, tools, woodwork and such that had been handled by the lepers before he touched them.   This degree of reasonable care taken, he seems not to have feared the disease for himself, even with all his close hourly contact with the sufferers.   At one time he spoke, in a letter to Mrs. Semmes, of expecting to become a victim, but happily he was mistaken.

Happily for himself, for his work, and—not least— for Father Damien.   Already stricken with leprosy at the time Brother Joseph came, Damien knew how short a time there was left for him.   And here, at last, was a man with whom he could get along amicably and on whom he could depend.   Gradually Dutton took over the management of most of Damien's affairs, and also served as carpenter, stonemason, architect and landscape gardener in addition to his nursing and secretarial work.

On the day after his arrival Dutton set to planning the new bathing establishment. He had brought with him from Honolulu the drugs used in the Japanese treatment that Damien was interested in, and now he started to arrange these and to build the bath-house needed for the warm baths that were a part of the cure. This work he did himself, working far into the night so that Damien might the sooner proceed with the treatment. But we know already that it not only failed to help him but may indeed have hastened his end. His restlessness grew on him as this final period drew to a close.

"As things first occurred to him he would take his cue, and off he was, to use his most frequent expression. 'Off I am, Brother Joseph!' he said to me daily, almost hourly, and always with the request that I finish what he was doing when the new project was suggested that called him off; that is, if it was a thing I could do, as usually it was. He seldom came back to the old jobs. By the time he finished, or before, something different would be quite likely to carry him to fields not thought of before. And then would come the expression, 'Brother Joseph, you are going to finish these'—referring to the previous jobs. And he would laughingly add, 'I am the carpenter, Brother Joseph the joiner.' With me it was an almost constant finishing of jobs he started—carpenter, joiner, and various sorts of things—everything. My boyhood familiarity with tools and my having been in charge of army construction work served me well in those busy years. Very useful to me (and to him).''

The moment Damien learned that his new assistant had had experience in construction work in the Army, a great building project leaped into his mind. Though it was not to come to full fruition in the priest's lifetime, yet a start was made in constructing a new church and some new houses and in putting through repairs. A modern kitchen, too, was built, and the conditions under which the lepers' food was prepared were substantially improved under Dutton's direction. In time this supervision was taken over by the Government, with yet greater improvements; but this did not come until after Damien's death.

"He was always rushing about. Yet, in his rushing way, he almost always stayed long enough to get my views about any kind of building work. It should be added that very little of the work done by Father Damien was wholly useless, though it was taken up hurriedly and carried out with the help of others. He had a way with his own work and with the aid of others—a way of making things turn out all right, at least so that a thing would work, though very often it would be far different from what he had first intended. Sometimes the result would be amusing, but he would say, 'Well, we can use it!' He always had great zeal and was ready to pursue with vigor whatever it seemed to him ought to be done. And he rather expected others to take his view. It made no difference whether it was his duty to do it; anything that he thought was good to do was for his immediate action—he considered that it became his duty."

Before Joseph Dutton came to the colony he had spent a good deal of time wondering whether he would find enough to do there. It needed not more than a few days, as we have seen, for his doubt to be answered emphatically. There were so few hands to do anything, and so much that was crying to be done. He worked often until half-past one or two o'clock in the morning; "though," he adds, "I rise every morning at four-thirty as is my usual habit." The evenings that were not spent in work were used for writing letters to friends or for reading the newspapers from America.

The two churches that Father Damien had put under his care constituted another responsibility, even though he had no priestly functions. "Aided him in serving the masses and in assisting about the various ministrations as far as a layman could." Yet he seems always to have been doubtful whether he was worthy to serve mass; he could not forget that he had turned his back on his world because of sinfulness, and to his dying day he wondered whether he had been forgiven.

The orphan leper children who were continually being sent to the colony were one of Damien's tenderest cares. Frightened and lonely they came, friendless until taken under the protection of the kindly priest. Often they were quite little children, and these were put into the orphanage that Damien had built. True, it hardly merited the name, being only a cluster of rude huts and cabins grouped around the priest's house. But what comfort and joy could be brought into the children's lives, Father Damien took great pains to bring. There was a school of sorts, with such teachers as he could find in the settlement. A choral society had been organized among the boys, and even a band. A visitor who saw this band has left a description of it, whose details may be overdrawn but whose general atmosphere is probably veracious:

"It was strange indeed to see these musicians, all of them lepers. Several had only two fingers on their hands. The organist at Kalawao had but one hand, and even that was maimed; he had fastened to what remained of his left hand a stick, and with that he struck the bass notes. Once, in the middle of a piece, I saw a musician lose part of his finger, and part of a lip drop off. Several were blind, but it did not matter, for they loved music, and Father Damien loved to hear them play."

Horrible? Yes. It has not been the object of this book to emphasize or to bring into the foreground the physical results of leprosy; they are for the most part indescribable, and the reader must be asked to take them for granted. But it is through an occasional and casual bit of hideousness such as the one above that we are made to realize something of what the two

Samaritans encountered (and handled) every day and every hour of their lives on Molokai. We are here reading not of a merely tragic and fatal epidemic such as the "flu," but of what is probably the vilest disease ever known to humanity. And it is. only when we begin to realize the implications of leprosy in its advanced stages that we can appreciate the character and the service of the men who ministered to the lepers.

Presently the care of the orphan boys was handed over to Brother Joseph, and a great load of responsibility was thus lifted from Damien's shoulders. "I can die now," he said, shortly before his death, "knowing that Brother Joseph will care for my orphans."

We have spoken of his increasing nervousness as death drew near. This showed itself not only in his impatience to be at fresh jobs but also in actual bad temper. Other assistants, earlier, had encountered this temper, and had left. But with Brother Joseph—patient, equable Brother Joseph—it was otherwise. Not only did he have no quarrels with the priest; they seem to have become warmer friends as time went on.

"The good understanding between us was positive and actual. There were times when one did not care to be too much with Father Damien—that must be said. But there was love between us. This is not to say that our tastes and personal habits were the same; it would not be correct to say that. Everyone has some repugnances, and in taking up this new life I found, as I expected, many things naturally repugnant, very different. I was firm in one resolve—to get along with

everyone and everything. . . . If my intimate association with him was longer than others' it was partly
because I admitted my own faults, partly because I
always saw him place in me the most entire confidence
and have in his heart a deep love, no matter what his
exterior appearance might be. Also, I used to be quite
open with him in speaking of all these things; he likewise with me; and this seems to have given us confidence in each other."

It is not too much to say, evidently, that Joseph Dutton had a remarkable character: humble, patient, even-
tempered, wise in his dealings with a difficult man.
Dr. Mouritz wrote: "Dutton had a divine temper;
nothing could ruffle it. No vulgar or angry speech
ever emanated from his lips, nothing could make him
angry; and the more work that fell to his lot the better
he liked it."

One shadow, and one only, lay between the two
men. Damien, for the first time since coming to
Molokai, now had someone to talk to as a friend,
someone with whom to spend long evenings in easy,
friendly conversation. And in the course of these
talks he was given to urging Dutton to become a priest.
Now Dutton was perfectly willing to tell anything that
Damien wanted to know about America, the country
that the priest had never seen, even to tell him of his
own past experiences. But certain things in his past
that he considered insuperable objections to his taking
orders, these he could not discuss; and the argument
always filled him with discomfort.

BROTHER JOSEPH AND OTHER BROTHERS. KALAWAO, MOLOKAI, MAY, 1905

"For several months Father Damien urged me to become a priest, with such insistence that it was one of the hardest trials of my life. Had I been fit, it might have been different. But the priesthood requires high character and great purity. I was not fit to be a priest or under vows and serve at the altar, and his request bothered me greatly (though no doubt it was a trial permitted for my good). I could not, for certain reasons, tell him why I was not fit to become a priest. Later, however, I did. He ceased at once speaking about it."

In return for the confidences that eventually came, Damien told his assistant the story of his own childhood and some details of his early life. Dutton, in one of his letters to Frank Waterbury, gives a summary of that evening's talk:

"Father Damien one evening gave me his confidence, telling of his boyhood and of his long desire to become a priest. I judged that the farm in Belgium was a poor one and the family without much means. Told of his early schooling and later study, and it seemed to me—though perhaps one should not judge— that he was not so well prepared as other priests. A brother, Pamphile, was to come to the Island as missionary, but, while he was in a hospital with fever, Damien begged to be allowed to take his place. This was granted and he came to the Islands, where the world knows his record. Was much interested in his account of [his] early life. Seemed to have always been one who saw ahead his true vocation. Would never call him a scholar, though he told me that he received private instruction in Latin from his brother Pamphile and in a few months was able to enter the theological school.   Later came schooling in Paris. Said it was God's act that caused him to ask if he could take his brother's place."

The two men had a hint that over on the larger Island there was a rich Protestant business man who was prepared, sooner or later, to build and equip a home for the Molokai leper boys.   And this prospect —though it was not to materialize for some years— fired Damien and Dutton to set about making plans. Besides the new houses that were already built or started, they began clearing away the stones from the site of what is now the Baldwin Home.   The ground was then covered with ugly rocks, and was bare of trees.   But the two men had vision—this place was to be covered with buildings and shaded by plenty of trees—and at once they began to realize that vision.

It is no exaggeration to say that for both of them all this constituted the happy life.   Dutton might be working hard, and spending many hours at loathsome service for his lepers; Damien might be entering months of horrible suffering with certain death at their end.   But everything written or said by either man during these three years breathes satisfaction and peace.   Damien was seeing his work grow and conditions improve for the lepers in his care.   Dutton was finding spiritual rest in working out his penance. "Since my fortieth birthday in 1883," he wrote, "I have always felt like one under probation, though not actually so regarded by the Church. Felt like one coming under its penitential system, always feeling a penitent; and the sacrament of penance is part of the Christian life."

Such a passage disproves once and for all the suspicions that have been voiced about the reality of Brother Joseph's conversion. It was a complete surrender, and it satisfied his heart and his mind. He brought to the Church's creed and ritual the calm and simple faith of a child. It is this attitude that explains the intense reverence he had for the office of his co-worker. As a man Damien might be disorderly and unclean, erratic and ill-tempered, utterly impossible for the average person to get along with pleasantly; but as priest he commanded deference and honor.

"There is one thing more important than any other in dealing with the character of Father Damien: he was a priest, a minister of God. The important thing is his priesthood; his private character has nothing to do with it. He was in many ways a good priest, a good man. He was very devout, and in his tranquil moments seemed to take a supernatural view of things —I may say of almost everything. His morning meditation was generally of about an hour's duration, and he had a regular practice of paying a visit to the Blessed Sacrament at night before going to bed. He offered the Holy Sacrifice long after he seemed unable to do so, and recited his offices nearly to the last, indeed for some time after being dispensed and while his eye was hardly able to see. The sight of one eye, he told me, was ruined in childhood; and toward the end he had to use many devices to be able to see at all with the other. For nearly a year it gave him great pain. It seemed to me [that] the recitation of his offices under those circumstances showed marked heroism. He suffered very greatly in his last year."

Damien was dying, and the realization spurred him on to fresh energy. The new church that was being built needed much work before it could be finished, and he was straining every nerve and muscle to complete it before death should overtake him. At his side was Brother Joseph, wielding hammer and saw, tugging at stones for the masonry. Again and again he urged his superior to spare himself, but to no avail. "All who noted his efforts in those last few weeks will join me in asserting that these extra exertions considerably hastened his end. Rest he would not, nor did he make any complaint about his condition."

Toward the end both men were cheered by the long-awaited arrival of more helpers. We have told of the priests who came, and of the Sisters who opened a girls' orphanage of a very much better kind than the crude house that had been in charge of a few unskilled leprous women. At the head of the three Franciscan nuns from Syracuse was a remarkable woman, Mother Marianne, their Provincial. She was to labor at Molokai for thirty years before death came, and was one of Brother Joseph's warmest friends. He held her in the deepest reverence, and long after she died he treasured some tiny and exquisite greeting cards that she had made. A year before her death he wrote:

"Mother Marianne is a wonderful woman, and is gaining strength. I really believe she is trying to do as I asked her years ago—not to die before me, as I would not go to her funeral but would pray for her from the other side of the little peninsula. My meaning she appreciates, for she well knows one's limits when under voluntary penance as I am."

Her desire to survive Brother Joseph was not, however, to be granted; she died in 1918 at the age of eighty, and Brother Joseph was to live for thirteen years longer. In 1920 he gave $120 from his funds toward a monument to her memory.

In Father Damien's last days the nervousness left him and he became quiet and calm. Dutton speaks thus of this period:

"His feeling toward me, his confidence, was touchingly exhibited at his death. When dissolution was evidently near, and the Fathers had come, he asked them to leave all his effects and money accounts for me to put in order and settle, which I did. Father Damien died on April 15, 1889. This death, after such a life, arrested the world's attention. A spontaneous outburst of applause from everywhere followed at once. The sixteen years of labor on Molokai made a record that is unique. The world knew very little about lepers. This was a revelation and was

recognized as heroic self-sacrifice. He is acknowledged
as the Apostle of the Lepers, and whatever others may
do in the same field will help to perpetuate his fame
and honor."

.    .    .    .    .    .    .

"His life and sacrifice are the things we must never
forget. He never spared himself, and in the end died
for those he loved. He made Molokai known to the
world."

Brother Joseph had been named, with a priest, as
executor of Father Damien's estate. This was only
natural. It was he who had been closest to Damien
in these last years, he who rounded the earth above his
friend's grave, he who went through all the personal
effects of the dead man. But when the Catholic Mission wanted him to come to Honolulu in connection
with settling the estate, he asked to have someone on
the main Island put in his place; he did not want to
visit civilization again. His wish was respected.

But there was much to do before he could turn the
final records over to the bishop. Father Damien had
kept all the letters that came to him from England,
the letters sent by the subscribers to the Chapman
Fund raised for the leper mission. There were several hundred of these, many of them from persons of
note and title. Joseph wrote:

"All expressed the greatest admiration for the priest.
They were packed, I remember, in one of the Japanese
medicine boxes; and thus packed they went to the

bishop, as did also the decoration bestowed on Father Damien by the King of Hawaii. The other effects were turned over to Father James, who was one of the executors. At my request the courts made a change, as I did not wish to go to Honolulu."

Brother Joseph was practically never, indeed, to leave the confines of the mission until he was dying some forty years after this; and when the Baldwin Home was built and its grounds enclosed, he refused to leave the enclosure. He made only two exceptions to this resolution, one of them being explained thus:

"In 1893 the Fathers here and in Belgium asked me again to take Damien's effects and put them in order, and after fumigation to send them to the Damien Institute near Louvain, Belgium; making a complete descriptive list, with my certificate as to actual use, by him, of every article—some [for] personal use, and others belonging to church and used by him: church ornaments, books, etc. This was requested because these articles were in my charge before and after Father Damien's death, and there was no other one living who could testify as to the actual use. I went to Kalaupapa, April 15, 1893, to complete the putting of these things in order. This was my last visit to Kalaupapa (about two miles away). In Father Damien's lifetime I had been with him to Kalaupapa two days each week. After his death I had little occasion to go, save to attend to these effects. And then came on the construction of the new home here, the Baldwin Home. My hands were full of the routine work, care of the sick, the dressing, and the working of the new home construction. Since the day I took the effects to Kalaupapa I have not been away from the home grounds here at Kalawao."

There is a story—pretty but quite untrue—that gained some credence after Father Damien's death. It is to the effect that after the funeral Brother Joseph climbed the dangerous path that wound up through the cliffs behind the settlement, and sat down when he reached a high eminence. Far below him he saw the trees and the huts of the colony, and before him stretched the glittering waters of the Pacific Ocean. Over all lay a deep silence. And he began to think; he sat there for hours, it was said, looking off toward where Honolulu lay below the horizon. What he was trying to decide was whether he should go on with his penance, or return to America and take up his life once more in the world of men.

It is a dramatic tale, but it is belied by every word that Joseph Dutton wrote about his feeling toward his Molokai life. He did not regret entering the colony—he never once thought of leaving it. As for climbing the cliffs, he says, "I have never left the grounds here; and though behind me are the cliffs, I have never been to the top, or away from the yard of the Baldwin Home since April 15, 1893." Instead of wanting to get away into the larger world, he wished indeed to make his own world yet smaller than it had been before.

"As the years passed, I found that the situation precisely conformed to my idea of reparation that brought

BROTHER JOSEPH AND LEPER BOYS

me here—to help my neighbor and fill out the primitive Church penance; making this my penitentiary, a
happy one for the ragged remnant of the years of life.
All officials have respected my feelings in this.  A dear
friend—one of the dearest on the Islands, or anywhere,
for that matter—had suggested a vacation years ago,
when my health was failing; even urging it, quite unable at first to see that nothing else would make me so
miserable.  It is so hard to understand the needs and
desires of others!"

And then follows a paragraph that deserves red letters, considering that he was talking of a place that
most of his fellowmen would regard as a living hell:

"Seek a vacation?  Why, I have a vacation all the
time, every blessed moment of the time, every moment
of all these blessed years, in doing what I like, what I
think my soul needs.  Anything else would be slavery.
Loafing around would make me miserable.  As it is,
I am enchanted.  The people here like me, I think,
and I am sure I like them."

And again, at the close of his life:

"Not for all the money men could count would I
leave my home here.  It has been a happy place—a
happy life."

# CHAPTER XII

## IN HARNESS

FATHER DAMIEN's death brought hundreds of letters flooding in to the settlement from all over the world, and it was the need of responding to their generous friendliness that compelled Brother Joseph to break through his early resolution against letter-writing. The first weeks of the new régime were filled to over-flowing with old duties and new; for though he had more helpers than there had ever been before, and Damien's priestly functions were now in other and competent hands, yet none of the newcomers were so familiar with the daily management of the colony as was Brother Joseph. A noteworthy episode of the re-organization period was the visit of Robert Louis Stevenson, which has been briefly described in an earlier chapter. We may quote here the two notes of reminiscence left by Brother Joseph, who was his guide during the visit of somewhat more than a week.

"The doctor had mentioned to me that some writer was at Kalaupapa, but I paid no attention to it. So when Mr. Stevenson called at our old place [I] did not know who he was, as no one told me. I was busy, and he looked for someone to show him over the place—the old home—[but] saw no one suitable. The crowd with me were having sores dressed. Mr. Stevenson looked very cool and pleasant in yachting cap and suit; name on capband was *Casco*. I said he would have to take me.

"He was on a horse and dismounted, and we went over the place together and saw the bad cases. He was sympathetic and highly interested, and showed it in feeling and expression. Highly strung organism and temperament, quick to feel, quick to love—a very affectionate disposition. Seemed as if he had not completed his plans. He was looking for a place to end his days—weak, ill. Inquired as to danger of contracting leprosy here; how it would be advanced with other disease. He knew, of course, his physical condition; I could judge only partly. His objects were only suggested, but when I knew later who he was and more of him, these thoughts seemed clear—that he was going to put himself somewhere to spend his dying years.

"I observed the same earnest desire that had been a feature of my own aim and hungry search for what might be my greatest good while trying to do good for others. Looked over the old place—quaint and strange to him, quaint to me now as memory goes back to those days. Walked and looked, seeing and sympathizing with all the sick and advanced cases. We talked even to the time of his departure. Remounting the horse and slowly working toward the gate, he seemed more and more interested, and with consummate skill drew from me the motives that controlled my coming here. He showed a deep sympathy with these motives and inquired very particularly as to the life here.

When I heard he had located at Samoa, the thought came back that he was 'looking around.' Considering his family, he could hardly have settled here, even if he had thought of it."

Here again, it will be noted, is variation from Brother Joseph's descriptions elsewhere of Stevenson's visit, owing probably to the confusion of an old man's memory. He mentions also two letters that he had later from Stevenson—letters that cannot now be found. "Mr. Stevenson wrote that he had not been able to forget the scenes he saw on his visit to Molokai, and would remember them till death." And—"Stevenson sent me his defense of Damien, which, though harsh, seems justified. He became a worshiper of the Father while he was on his visit here." And Stevenson himself, in the letter to Dr. Hyde, was to give his impression of the place in these words:

"I do not think I am a man more than usually timid; but I never recall the days and nights I spent upon that island promontory without heartfelt thankfulness that I am somewhere else. I find in my diary that I speak of my stay as a 'grinding experience'; and when the *Mokolii* bore me at last towards the outer world I kept repeating to myself, with a new conception of their pregnancy, those simple words of the song:

" ' 'Tis the most distressful country that ever yet was seen.' "

Not long after Damien's death one of the most-needed additions to the colony's equipment was begun

—the boys' orphanage called the Baldwin Home, fruit of the generosity of Henry P. Baldwin, a wealthy sugar-planter of Maui. The Board of Health appointed Brother Joseph as its manager and put absolute authority into his hands. Twenty-five years before, when Father Damien first took charge of the settlement, the home for the leper orphans had been started with one primitive grass hut; when Brother Joseph died, the institution devoted to the care of the boys covered acres of ground, consisted of more than fifty buildings, and was one of the best-equipped plants of its kind in the world. Let him tell how it grew:

"It was, when I first came, just a little cluster of shanties and cabins scattered around his house. In 1886 Father Damien had some twenty or thirty of the lepers living near his house; in 1887 we had sixty, in 1904 there were a hundred and twenty. The cluster of little cabins did not answer the purpose very long. In 1887 it began to spread, and we built two houses of considerable size. This enlargement was sufficient as to capacity up to 1890—in fact, we had to do with it until May, 1894. But it was somewhat patchwork and not suitable for complete operation. Therefore, in 1890, we began to discuss a new and better home.

"In 1890-1-2 (along there) starts were made for our new home, but for one reason or another little progress was made. I was quiet at my work, not wishing any change; but Mr. W. O. Smith, then president of the Board of Health, took a notion in his head in 1893 to get me to take hold of the construction of the home, as Mr. Baldwin would supply the means. I told him I could carry it out if left entirely in my hands and not bothered, and so it was. Neither the Board of Health nor anyone else asked anything about the plans. I called for anything and everything that was needed; no one made any suggestions or asked any questions.

"The home was occupied in May, 1894. Soon after, the Board of Health came to see it. Everyone was astonished to see the old rock-pile turned into what it was. There was so much praise that I was almost ashamed, having come here to be a servant."

Not only did Mr. Baldwin furnish the money for the first buildings; until his death at sixty-nine, in 1911, he gave money again and again for improvements to the Home. But it is truly quite as much a monument to Brother Joseph's tireless planning and labors as to Mr. Baldwin's generosity. The site had originally been a barren rock-pile, treeless and covered with rubbish. Brother Joseph, with the help of such of the lepers as could work, removed the rocks and the rubbish after weeks of hard work, at a time when the Home itself was only a vision in the future; and in 1903 he was to write that he had planted the grounds with 5,000 eucalyptus trees that were doing well. The pride he took in the place is revealed in the letter in which he compares it with the girls' orphanage:

"Bishop Home is very pretty. This is the home for girls built near the steamer landing, the gift of Mr. Bishop of Honolulu and placed under the care of the Sisters. But the site does not compare with this.

Their houses are bunched closely, and the other houses are too near. For beauty of site, and general outline, there is not any place in the settlement to compare with ours here—at least, everyone says so. Mr. Stevenson called our place—the whole leper colony—a bracket on the wall; that gives the best idea. Two miles along the wall, projecting into the ocean, one mile in the middle part, like a dish or a bracket; a great depth of wall below the sea-surface and extending above the surface for at least 2,200 feet. All irregular cliffs, but very steep.

"The steamer landing is at Kalaupapa and, since the water-pipes have been carried over there, it has become the largest part of the colony because the administration buildings were moved there. Our Home has about one-half of the Kalawao population. It is a beautiful place, indeed the most beautiful in the world —I can think of none better."

The appointment of Brother Joseph as manager of the Baldwin Home created some friction and jealousy. At the time he went to the Island the leper colony was under the control of the Board of Health, as it had always been. But, owing to the magnitude of Father Damien's service and the publicity that his death won for the colony, the impression spread that it was controlled by the Church. The Catholic Church, however, had not been favored above any other faiths—many denominations had missions among the lepers; and when the Baldwin Home was opened and it was learned that the officials were not putting it under Church control but into Brother Joseph's hands personally, there was a good deal of protest. Dutton himself explains the situation thus:

"It may be well to state what the Hawaiian Government has to do with both the Home and the settlement, and explain the general relations of the Government with the leper settlement as a whole. There has been much misapprehension on this point, mostly because there has been more published about Father Damien than about the Government, leaving the impression that he was in charge of the settlement and had made all the improvements—an incorrect impression. It has always been operated by the Board of Health of the Hawaiian Government. The regular and general expenses are paid by the Government, including a ration of clothing and food for each leper. At first many lepers built their own cabins, but more recently the Government has constructed a number of good cabins. It builds all now. It did build the residence of one of the priests, but otherwise the mission, located on Government ground, has paid its own expenses.

"The expense for construction of the home for girls at Kalaupapa was principally borne by a charitable Protestant gentleman in Honolulu, Mr. Bishop. The Government operates it as it does the boys' home here, giving the Sisters support. This place is very much isolated, and if in the earlier years the conditions were unsatisfactory, I believe—I know, in fact— that the Hawaiian Government ought not to be blamed. There are many drawbacks which would

BROTHER JOSEPH IN THE GARDEN NEAR HIS COTTAGE

always tend against a rapid improvement.  But considering the nature of the people to be dealt with, it would appear that the Government has given it good support.

"Of course, after the territory was taken over by the United States there came a marked advance in conditions; this would be expected.  The general outfit now is completed, with establishments for medical departments, hospitals, etc.  There are bath-houses. Two Catholic churches, two Protestant, and one of the Mormon faith.  The appropriation by Congress was generous, and we have everything science can give. A great change since 1903."

Though this passage carries us ahead of the story it clarifies the official status of the colony, which was so vaguely understood by those who expected that the Baldwin Home would be put into the hands of the Church.  Though the Board of Health did not do this, it did decide that the best persons to look after the boys directly were the Brothers who were expected to arrive soon after the opening, and who were to be paid for their services.  But the whole was to be —this was clearly understood—under the direction of Brother Joseph, who, though he reported nominally to the superintendent of the colony, was actually given almost absolute authority.

The jealousy roused by his appointment seems to have emanated chiefly from one man, who had been practically sent away from the colony and who got the idea that his dismissal was the doing of Brother Joseph

and the president of the Board of Health.  The stories
that he proceeded to circulate about the colony, in
newspapers, weeklies, and public addresses, were quite
untrue, but they troubled Brother Joseph little.  Once
only did he mention the matter.  "I am always sorry,"
he writes, "for a jealous man, and one who, blinded
by rage, finds it impossible to see the truth."

There was, however, no other friction in the management of the Home.  The facts that he was a layman
and that he had conspicuous ability in organization
were recognized by the officials, and he was to continue
as its head for thirty-six years.

The boys in the Home, who seem to have numbered some 150 on an average, were either orphans
of lepers or the leprous children of parents who stayed
at their homes on other Islands.  Besides these the inmates included men who had become totally or partly
helpless in advanced stages of leprosy.  The rules of
the Home are simple.  All boys of less than eighteen
years who are not under the care of parents or
guardians must enter the Home and remain until they
are eighteen.  They may then leave if they are able
to prove to the superintendent that they can care for
themselves.  While they are in the Home they may
not leave its grounds without permission; and Brother
Joseph says that this was not granted without sufficient
reason.  Visitors must get permission to see the place;
but visitors seldom came, since it was the policy of the
Board of Health not to encourage them except with
good reason.  The superintendent of the settlement

was supposed to make a weekly tour of inspection, though this was not done regularly.

The Brothers who had charge of these boys and men were paid $25 a month by the Government; and each one turned his pay-check over to the Catholic mission. Brother Joseph received no salary; and he wrote once—when during the World War it became necessary to cut down expenses—"The cut was nearly fifty percent, but I rather had the laugh on the officials, in that they could not cut me down because I have never accepted any pay at all."

In addition to the oversight of routine matters, disciplinary problems, and the task of beautifying the Home grounds, he presently undertook to provide recreation and amusement for the boys. Appeals for funds from private citizens of Maui resulted in the organization of various sorts of games, the purchase of a flag, and the institution of the band. Brother Joseph could always count on the help of Mr. Baldwin, who was a warm admirer, but he never appealed to him for the contributions that came so promptly until he had exhausted other possibilities. "Mr. Baldwin," he wrote, "was one of my best friends. He frequently reminded me to call on him for any special need here; and I do, once in a while, but not too often. It would not do to injure such a resource by too frequent calls, so when I do call he knows it is urgent and responds at once." Baldwin, on his side, remarked, "I never regret anything I do for you." And after Baldwin's death Brother Joseph commented, "No man ever did more real good than he did, and he will be rewarded."

The annexation of the Islands by his own country brought great joy to the lay brother. He had always been a passionate patriot, with a faith in our flag that made it a sacred thing to him. He always wrote of his country as though it were a living being of flesh and blood. One of the few speeches he ever indulged in during his life was made at the raising and dedication of the new flag at the Baldwin Home. He told the boys that the flag was the symbol of justice and freedom, of honor and good-will. A small card found among his keepsakes bears the picture of the flag and these words written below: "My little missionary." When in 1894 Henry Baldwin and others sent him money for band instruments, he refused to let the boys play them until a flag had been obtained and displayed on the flag-pole he had had erected on the grounds. A flag was hung above his desk in the little office. In many such ways he kept close to his heart the country from which he had voluntarily exiled himself.

A new policy resulted from the changed political status of Molokai. Another hospital was begun, and to it came a physician whose name is always to be famous in connection with the work of helping lepers. Before Dr. Goodhue's arrival little effort had been made to apply antiseptic surgery to the task of conquering the disease. The course of leprosy is not steady; often it breaks out in one sore, and then for years goes no farther, the patient remaining in good health otherwise. But hardly ever do such sores heal of themselves. In the case of an ulcer, when the bone is attacked necrosis sets in, and if this is not checked it will eat along the bone until the sufferer dies of gangrene. After Dr. Goodhue came he used surgery in such cases, removing the ulcer and cleaning the bone, so that the progress of the disease was at least halted for a time. But what was more important, an effort to find a cure was begun.

When Brother Joseph was asked whether he believed leprosy to be either infectious or contagious he replied:

"Yes and no—both answers can be given. To my mind leprosy is transmitted by what I would call a cycle of events. If the events occur in proper order—that is, if an individual receives certain toxins and in a certain way, a way that will produce certain combinations—the result will be leprosy. But the absence of any one of the events will prevent it. It's not infectious in the proper sense of the word, though no doubt it is feebly contagious. We know little about the matter, though we do know that association with lepers rarely means that one will have the disease. It's not curable, though there have been occasions when Nature seems to have checked its ravages. I doubt if there will ever be a cure—that is, a definite cure."

And in another letter we find this:

"There is much dispute about leprosy, but all authorities agree that if it is contagious it is but mildly so. There are many cases of non-lepers living many years with lepers and never being afflicted. Believed to be brought into the system through the mouth, and strange things have been done in attempts to infect animals with the germ. All attempts to inoculate dogs and other animals have failed. One instance where a human being was so inoculated was not considered satisfactory; the person did break out with the disease later, but it was shown that he had lived with lepers before and had the disease in his family. The doctors and the Sisters here have not been afflicted, because of taking ordinary precautions. Few white people seem to be subject. I am careful, washing often; that is all. Those who deal with lepers daily, like doctors and Sisters, have no fear, knowing that the disease is but slightly infectious—or perhaps better, contagious."

But in his prophecy that there would never be a cure he was wrong, though when he wrote the words he was expressing what the world had believed for thousands of years. Much of the horror roused by leprosy has been due to the impotence of medical science to deal with it. It was not until 1910 that a new and more hopeful era opened. In India it had long been known that some relief could be obtained by the use of a derivative of the shrub *Taraktogenos kurzii,* chaulmoogra oil, and this oil had been used for thousands of years in treating leprosy. But few would take it because it was so nauseating. In 1914 Dr. Victor Heiser, of the United States Public Health Service, began to use it in transmuscular injections, which, however, proved to be long and very painful. The suffering consequent on these injections was so pronounced that not many lepers could be induced to undergo them. But it was observed that in many cases where they did submit, the disease appeared to be checked and the leper bacillus destroyed. Thus, though the new method represented an advance on the old capsule treatment, the Hawaiian Board of Health, through Dr. Hollman, set about finding a still better method. The experimental work was carried on by the Chemistry Department of the University of Hawaii, whose president delegated the task to a young Negro chemist, Alice Ball. What was sought was a more diluted form of the oil, free from useless matter. Miss Ball began her work under the direction of President Dean and, though her health broke down at once and she was forced to take a rest, she returned to her laboratory; she became ill a second time and died shortly. The president then took up her work at the point where she had laid it down, and after months of intensive research, for which costly apparatus had to be provided—and even invented—he succeeded in finding the precise ethyl ester for which he was searching. With this discovery a new day dawned for the lepers of the world.

The new treatment, which is far less painful and does not produce the horrible abscesses incident to the old, is the one used today at both Molokai and the hospital near Honolulu. Extravagant claims were made for it at first; what is recognized now is that chaulmoogra oil is a cure for leprosy within certain limits and for some cases.  Dr. Hollman is convinced that a definitive cure must be a slow process, that the germs often lie hidden and dormant for some time; and the rule today is that when a patient is thought to be cured he is put on parole and for several years must return for continued treatment.

But one gratifying effect the treatment is certainly having, which may result in the end in the abandonment of the leper colony: mild cases, those in the early stages, are given the treatment at the Kalihi hospital on the mainland instead of being sent at once to Molokai.  The idea is that every new case shall report at once to the hospital and there receive diagnosis and treatment, and that the need of actual segregation shall be reduced more and more.  Now, for the first time in the world's history, undoubted cases of leprosy have been pronounced cured, and few cases are called really hopeless.  Even though we must be cautious in our confidence in the effectiveness of this new treatment, and though we no longer are so enthusiastic about it as its exponents were in the beginning, yet we have the right to be more hopeful than our ancestors were of checking the scourge.

These experiments were watched with great interest, naturally, by Brother Joseph.  He wrote that, if they were successful, his Home would become simply a memory.

"Until about 1900 the natives here would not accept

THE LAST PICTURE OF BROTHER JOSEPH

any kind of treatment, as a rule, from what they called foreign doctors. It has been very hard to make them see the value of the new remedy, for they are not forced to take it or any remedy. In fact, here, even when they saw its results, one-half refused to take the cure. This is perhaps due to the sufferings of those who took the old treatment—the painful abscesses and the like. The present chaulmoogra oil derivative is a remedy within certain limits; that is, in the early stages and the mildest forms, in cases where the general health is good. So, in a good number of cases, a final cure can be expected.

"Looking back to 1886 a great change is noticeable now. The old-time hopeless, crippled, mutilated scraps of humanity, for whom the sore-dressing, poulticing, and heroic, rough surgery were used—these very sad cases are few as compared with the past. With better general care and scientific treatment few cases become hopeless. Perhaps some day they will cure every one, though I doubt it; but they are starting to cure some now. Perhaps the fight against leprosy has been won—at least, the front trenches have been taken."

But most of Brother Joseph's time was occupied with considerations far less arresting than these experiments. He himself thought of his days as uneventful, though every hour of them was filled with constructive work. Someone asked him once to set down the principal events of his management of the Baldwin Home, and he replied:

"There are none to write about. Each day was filled with its tasks. . . . Duties in general do not admit of many musings for me. I have just one time to think: Saturday mornings, when the overhauling and cleaning of my little cottage comes on—yes, and when the barbering is done once a month. But for the rest of my time, days and nights are like this. Mass—this always, of course. Some odd little matters first. Breakfast, then morning work; this for all hands able to be about and not employed with the sick. Cleaning grounds [by] gangs of sweepers, some of us running lawn-mowers, pickers, hand-cart and dirt-box gang. I always take a lead in this to set an example. Oh, yes—since wireless, after the Brothers have read the news I post it."

Though it was his habit to rise each day at four-thirty, this was sometimes not done simply because he had not gone to bed at all the night before. For as the years went on there was more and more letter-writing to be done, and his evenings were often so filled. "The clock now strikes 4 A.M., and not one-quarter of what I hoped to do is done. Must get my hot bath now before Mass. . . . *Later.* Hot bath is *pau* [Hawaiian for *finished*] and yet I have a little time before daybreak." He was eighty-four years old when he wrote this, and he was lamenting that there was not more time for all that he wanted to do.

If we are to realize all that he did get done we must pass from his letters to those written by the various presidents of the Board of Health, from the superin-

tendents of the colony, and from Dr. Goodhue. The
details covered in these letters range from food and
laundry, clothing and supplies, to problems of discipline; and all of them came to Brother Joseph for
decision. Many of the letters deal with his requisi-
tions for seeds, trees, and the other things he wanted
for improving the grounds. One series relates to his
desire to have a horse of his own. Why or when he
decided that he wanted one does not appear. There
were, of course, horses in the settlement, and trucks
and cars later. And since he never went outside the
Home grounds one may wonder what he wanted a
horse for. But evidently he got one, and presently it
fell sick of a throat infection. Brother Joseph was
much worried, particularly when Dr. Goodhue was
appealed to and failed to find out what was the matter
with the animal; which is hardly to be held against
him since he was no veterinary. So Brother Joseph
then decided to bring over a veterinary from the main
Island. Before the matter was settled finally the superintendent had written five letters about it, of from
three to four pages each. Dr. Goodhue having failed
him, three other doctors were called in with no more
success. As for the Honolulu veterinary, he must
come even if he had to stay over for the week between
steamer calls. Eventually the patient superintendent
wrote, when this last resort was proposed to him: "As
it will cost at least $12 a day for this man's services,
and as your poor animal is not worth much over $30,
it would be cheaper to shoot him and get a new one."

Brother Joseph's marginal comment on this suggestion is: "I should have thought of this." We may assume that it was settled thus.

These marginal comments in his close, fine handwriting throw some light on his way of handling details. There were the bags of flour that arrived spoiled; he reported the matter. On the superintendent's reply ("I would certainly say you had grounds for complaint") he notes: "Did not make any complaint. Merely stated facts. The flour was spoiled." His friend Mr. Smith suggested that he should take a vacation: "It would do you good to come away for a short time and have the rest you have earned." "No, sir!" is the red-ink retort. He organized a baseball league and asked for twenty-four balls; he got two, and puts a big question-mark after the *two*. There are the letters dealing with an inmate who had insulted one of the Brothers. The superintendent waxed eloquent over what *he* would have done with the offender: "The priest should have pulled a picket off the fence and broken it over his head!" "Maybe," comments Brother Joseph; "but I don't like my fence spoiled."

All the letters from the various superintendents testify to the warm friendliness that subsisted between them and the lay brother. In the five hundred and more that have come to us there is only one complaint, the writer apologizing for reporting that the food in the Home had been criticized. Brother Joseph said nothing, but only sent the superintendent a complete list of the foods used during the previous years, with the amounts of each; and this ended the discussion.

As the history of the colony approaches our own day we note many respects in which Brother Joseph's task was lightened and the condition of his lepers improved. By 1923 the equipment was up-to-date, sanitary conditions ideal, and doctors and nurses adequate. Many of the lepers were earning a good living by their fishing. Automobiles were to be seen at the Kalaupapa boat-landing, and there were moving pictures and radios. (As for the radios in the Baldwin Home, however, they furnished little pleasure to Brother Joseph. "I once tried to listen, but it was no use—my deafness prevented a sound.") The colony was no longer the hell that it had once been called; it had become the finest leper colony in the world, and the Public Health Service provided it with the best medical care and treatment that were available.

Comments on this contrast fill Brother Joseph's letters during this last period of his life. "Things have changed here. It is a beautiful place now, and very modern." At eighty-four he recorded that he had cared for 1370 lepers in the Home since its opening. He had been its manager from the beginning, and there was not to be another until after he died. From time to time there were rumors that he had contracted leprosy; even, once, that he was dead. The truth is that until 1928 he was in perfect health. In January of that year he wrote: "Though weaker, I want to keep my harness on to the end. My life is on the downward slope, but I assure you it is a bright and happy slope, filled with sunshine. I hope to end my days in my Home here." He had seen many another wish granted, but in this one he was to be disappointed.

# CHAPTER XIII

## "LIFE HAS BEEN GOOD TO ME HERE!"

BROTHER JOSEPH's unwillingness to leave the leper colony was to be interrupted by two exceptions only. While the world went on as usual he had no desire to revisit it; he was happier where he was. But presently the world went to war, and then all his old fighting spirit surged up again. He had served his country in the Civil War, and now, old though he was, he must be off to fight with it in the World War. His proposal is surely one of the most astonishing phenomena of our part in that struggle. To W. O. Smith, the old friend who was president of the Hawaiian Board of Health, he wrote:

"I wanted to help organize quickly a few hundred of the old veterans, such of us as would be willing to close our days in this way; to coax Mr. Wilson to rush us to the front as a body of independent sharpshooters, needing no drill, no physical examination, no pay, of course, outfitting ourselves in the old blue uniforms. Not that we would do much good at the front—the Army would be stumbling over us; but for the example to the youngsters at home. It would have been painful for me, breaking away from such deeply rooted affections; nothing but the country's service

239

could cause me to go away or break the lines set for
voluntary penance.  Just as the War came I thought
to test myself.  If able to volunteer the third time [I]
could not be mustered in, of course, nor paid, being
more than double the age; but could do some special
duty in the field.  So I dropped the grooming—as I
called it: the baths, some old hurts that have to be
looked at—this I do at night.  After I did this, I knew
I could not be taken into the field—knew it two weeks
before my set time was up."

Here is the same sort of noble pathos, of reluctant
acceptance of defeat, that marked Theodore Roosevelt's passionate ambition to head a division of former
Rough Riders when we had declared war on Germany.
Both volunteers were brought to realize that their
proposals were not practicable, both were keenly disappointed.  It is hard to imagine what would have
happened to these few hundred men of the Grand
Army of the Republic, all of them over seventy, don-
ning their faded blue uniforms and rushed to the
front for the sake of the example they would set to
their grandsons.  But to Brother Joseph this was no
bizarre idea; it was a highly serious proposal.  Once
before, something like it had entered his head.  When
we were having trouble on the Mexican border and
the President sent Funston and Pershing there,
Brother Joseph read the news, and the thrill it evoked
produced an idea.

"When President Wilson made a landing at Vera
Cruz, I felt like buckling on my sword and haversack

At Eastertide

To honor Christ, Our Risen
Lord,
The Easter lilies bloom;
Oh may He send you joys as
sweet
As live in their perfume.

Easter Joys
be Jours.

To

From

THE LAST CARD SENT BY BROTHER JOSEPH

and going forth.   But at last I remembered that I was twice the age—three times, in fact—and could not go as in '61.   Ah, the heart stays young, but the body becomes unfit for serious soldiering.   Yet, if I could go, I would break my rule and leave here, though nothing else could make me."

No pacifist, Brother Joseph.   He had seen war, and to him it appeared as not so momentous an affair as a man's war within his own soul.   Once he wrote: "War is not pleasant, but there are times when it is cleaner than civilian life."

But if he was not to be allowed to make the dramatic and glorious gesture of his ambition, other services to his country lay within his power.   There were Liberty Bonds to be bought.   At the close of 1917 he had $1000 in a Honolulu bank, the last of the money he had brought with him from the States.   Of his funds in 1886 more than $10,000 had been given to charity, and of this remaining thousand he used the interest for buying Christmas gifts for the Sisters at the Bishop Home.   It had been his intention to bequeath the principal to some charity at the colony, probably the Bishop Home, since the Baldwin Home was already well provided for.   But when his idea of serving as a soldier was disappointed, he withdrew the thousand and invested it in Liberty Bonds.   "Four hundred in now," he directed.   "Three of $200 each to go in later, as I am sure there will be three more."

Brother Joseph had almost no personal possessions. A few keepsakes he treasured for their associations, such as the sprig of a plant that came from his mother's grave. But when gifts were sent to him he turned them over, as a rule, to the various institutions at the colony. The G.A.R., which had already sent several flags, voted at one of its annual encampments to send him a typewriter. He thanked them for "your fine typewriter. It's in use here at the hospital doing fine work. Poor as I am in writing, I stick to a pen." The machine had been turned over to the Board of Health office in the hospital. So, too, when Edison sent him a phonograph and many records; he passed them on to the Home. Practically his only private possession was a fine pair of binoculars, and these he gave to the United States Government for use during the War. The letter acknowledging their receipt was written by Franklin Roosevelt, Assistant Secretary of the Navy, who told him they were in service on a battleship. They were returned to him when the War was over, with a certificate to that effect. Brother Joseph framed the certificate and it became one of his most cherished possessions; but he gave the glasses to a midshipman. He wrote once that he envied those glasses, with their "opportunity to be of service, while I am unable to do much at all in this time of need."

His eagerness to "do his bit" communicated itself to the lepers in the colony when he instituted a drive for Red Cross and War Saving Stamp contributions. Americans at home who managed these drives did not invariably find it easy to elicit the response they hoped for; and certainly no team-manager would have expected any sort of response here at Molokai, where the inhabitants were wretchedly poor almost to a man. But when Brother Joseph went around and talked of their Government's needs, they found that—though they might have no money—they could do all sorts of chores to earn some. Fingers went to work, torn, diseased, feeble fingers, lifting stones, clearing away rubbish, fishing. And with what they earned they bought War Savings Stamps to the amount of $3,000—*lepers!* —and subscribed nearly $6,000 to the Red Cross.

Only second in interest to the World War in Brother Joseph's life during recent years was the visit of the sixteen battleships sent around the world by President Roosevelt in 1908. After the fleet had sailed from Hampton Roads the President was told that Brother Joseph very earnestly hoped that it might be sent past Molokai, close enough to the leper colony so that his people might see it. At once Roosevelt cabled to the ships to turn inland, on leaving Hawaii for Japan, and to sail past Molokai in battle formation.

And so, on a day of brilliant sunshine, the gallant ships of the United States Navy steamed slowly past the little promontory by the Home and dipped their flags to the watcher at the water's edge—a proud and happy exile on this day. Surrounded by his eager leper boys, he was already waiting when the first dim shadows rose above the horizon; and he stayed until the long gray column had passed out of sight again. It is not hard for us to picture that erect old figure in its humble suit of blue denim, white hair and beard bright in the sunshine, tears in his eyes as he stood at salute, his heart touched to pride and joy. After it was over he wrote of his gratitude and appreciation; and put among his mementoes a highly prized photograph of Theodore Roosevelt, with the inscription, "To Brother Joseph, with all good wishes." In an article for a Honolulu newspaper he wrote:

"It is an object-lesson to us all, and may God bless everyone who had even a little to do with bringing about this great pleasure. Our gratitude is beyond expression—[I] am thinking mostly of myself. Did ever anyone deserve so little and get so much? Our abode has been called *Molokai the Blest*. It surely was, this day. I need a new dictionary to find words [in which] to give my thanks."

The visit of the fleet immediately brought a heavier mail and increased the amount of letter-writing imposed on him. But in none of these letters did he go into details about the sufferings of his people. To him it was still "the most beautiful place in the world, and I am fortunate to be here among fine people who like me." He was never able to get caught up in this correspondence, and we do not wonder when we look at his old address-book, with its hundred and twenty-five pages all filled close with the names of persons who wrote to him—nearly four thousand of them, living in all parts of the world. Every President since Roosevelt is listed, and many of the Cabinet officers. The names of physicians and scientists crowd those of writers, inventors, and clergymen. Black ink was used for entering the names, and red ink to record the dates on which he sent answers and the mementoes that he sometimes gave to correspondents. The little brown book is much thumbed, testifying to constant hard usage, but in spite of his industry Brother Joseph was to confess himself, shortly before his death, more than four hundred letters behind!

These were the years when he wrote until late every night, so busy over letters that—as he said—he had no time for smoking. "I did color two fine meerschaums in the States, and used to smoke corncobs when I first came here; but never do any more—takes too much time to fill and light, with all my correspondence to be answered." Toward the end of his life he was to save himself much of this labor by having a leaflet printed and sent to almost a thousand of his correspondents at once; the expense of this being met from the annual Christmas gift of a hundred dollars that came to him from four Honolulu friends. But there were still many old and intimate friends, and a few newer ones to whom he wrote long, personal letters.

An unsolicited letter came to him one day from President Harding, typical of Harding's warm kindliness.

"My dear Brother Joseph:

"At various times over many years now, my attention has been called to the splendid Christian service you have been rendering to the unfortunate members of the leper colony at Molokai. Only quite recently my attention was drawn to the fact that now, at the age of eighty, you are still carrying on this wonderful work and are still enjoying good health. It is difficult to feel that this is less than one of those miraculous compensations which come at times to men and women who make the supreme sacrifice. I think it cannot fail to be a lesson, a great inspiration to all who feel the urge to great human service.

"The other day a friend spoke of the work of Father Damien and yourself. I had known, through the writings of Robert Louis Stevenson, something about the story of Father Damien, and more recently of how you had carried that work forward after Father Damien's death. I do not know why I have been moved to write a letter to you. I know very well that those who do the great and self-sacrificing tasks of the world have to find their satisfaction in the work which comes to their hand. I am very sure that nothing I can say can possibly add to the satisfaction which you must feel in having thus carried on a service to the bodies and minds and souls of men and women, for which we will find few parallels. But it has seemed not improper, I hope not an intrusion, for me to say to you that your work is not unknown, is not unappreciated; that all over the world there are people who regard you and Father Damien as men whose lives have been well-nigh perfect examples of self-abnegation, sacrifice, and service. You have set for us a model which I wish might be raised up for the view and emulation of others, for it is in the selfless service of all our brothers that all of us must at last find the great satisfactions and consolations of this life.

"So I shall end as I began, by saying that I have realized how impossible it is for me to say anything which will add to the satisfaction which you must derive from the consciousness of a noble and chivalrous work thus splendidly performed. I hope you may be spared many, many more years to carry it forward; and it would be one of the great pleasures of my own official service if I might be able, at any time or in any way, to extend a helping hand or influence in behalf of yourself and of those to whom you have given your life.

Most sincerely yours,<br>
WARREN G. HARDING"

Brother Joseph's reply to this letter, which moved him all the more deeply for being unexpected, was written shortly before the President's death—less than a month before; and it is to be doubted whether Harding ever saw it.

"My dear Mr. President:

"It was a beautiful letter. . . . Am wishing to be really as good and useful as you think. Have done and am doing my bit to help the lepers and to keep things in order. But the service has done me good. . . . My main feeling is one of intense gratitude towards Almighty God for giving me this opportunity. . . . Am enclosing a little photo of my dear old mother for Mrs. Harding, and thanks to you, dear friend, for your good letter.

Yours cordially and joyfully,<br>
JOSEPH DUTTON"

How naïve and awkward is this man's writing, yet
can any of his readers deny the qualities of high sincerity and humility and kindliness that radiate from
every word he wrote?  Surely he was "cordially and
joyfully, Joseph Dutton," through all his days.

Not long after President Harding's letter came,
Dutton remembered that President Coolidge had
been born in Vermont, not far from Joseph's own
birthplace.  And so—though he was anything but the
kind of person who writes to those in high places
simply to bring himself to their attention—he decided
to write to Coolidge as a fellow-Vermonter.  He also
enclosed a picture of his mother, as he had done in the
other case.  In time there was an acknowledgment—
no long, warm, expansive letter such as Harding had
written, but still a letter, a Coolidge letter.  In three
lines the photograph was acknowledged with thanks.

Many of the letters Dutton received were from persons who wanted to come out and help; to these he
had to reply that though the offers made him happy,
there was now no such need for assistance as there had
been in the old days.  Others offered money; this he
refused, saying that the Territorial Legislature made
ample provision for all purposes.  "Everyone," he remarked, "thinks of the place as it was in Father Damien's time—as greatly in need of help.  Everything
is different now."  One well-known English writer, a
woman, pursued her correspondence with him to great
length, reiterating the impression that his life of service had made on her and urging him to let her come

IN HIS OFFICE AT THE COTTAGE

out as a worker. So insistent did she become that finally he had to tell her that if she wanted to give herself in service to humanity she did not even have to leave London.

There were crank letters, of course. One woman reported that God had told her to come to Molokai and spend her days at his side; it might even be better if they married; how could she get there? We may be sure that there was no delay in sending this reply, to the effect that nobody could come to Molokai without the permission of the Board of Health, and that it was seldom given. (If Brother Joseph had been a few years younger, and living in the United States, he would have recognized in his reply a perfect example of "passing the buck.") Still other correspondents offered alleged cures for leprosy. A "dry" fanatic begged him to come to America and tour the country for Prohibition. Brother Joseph replied by reminding him of the word *temperance*.

A really valued source of letters was that other aged laborer in behalf of suffering humanity, Mother Mary Alphonsa (Lathrop), daughter of Nathaniel Hawthorne, who on entering the Catholic Church had transformed her country estate, "Hawthorne," into a hospital for incurable cancer patients. She wrote extensively of her hopes and plans, and at one time asked Brother Joseph to come to New York and take charge of the city Home while she should be in the country. Though much touched, he was obliged to refuse. "I have chosen my work as a place of penance and feel that it would not do to leave."

But the group of correspondents who were nearest
his affections were the friends of his younger days,
whose birthdays he remembered with interesting souvenirs and pictures of himself. "I write to my old-
time friends, their widows, and the children, and no
doubt bother them by sending souvenirs. Always I
have wanted to share everything I have with someone
else. No doubt they wonder what to do with the bits
I send them; but if so, they never talk, and appear
grateful." He clipped newspaper items about his life
and work, and sent them to any that he thought might
be interested. And evidently he did not always read
the items through, as illustrated in what happened in
September, 1926, when he sent to the Rev. John G.
Dutton of Agawam, Massachusetts, a biography of him
that had appeared in nine installments in a Catholic
paper. "I have not read this," he wrote, "though I
have been told it's flattering. Think it may interest
you." If he had read it he would have discovered how
many of its "facts" were inaccurate, if not actually
false.

He was never to feel very happy over the device of
broadcasting a printed letter rather than writing individual answers. It seemed to him a little cold and
unfriendly. But he had to come to it:

"It has become too much for pen alone, and I cannot see very clearly any more. How will it work, I
wonder, this new-fangled manner of correspondence—
a bit of printing and a few written words on each—?

When I take up a package to answer nowadays, it's very often I find eight or ten letters which I have not replied to. Even giving half the night to answering them has not brought me into line. If this plan works, I may keep it up, perhaps a year or two, Easter and Christmas. Am wishing to manage so that I will not lose a single correspondent. I cannot afford that sort of loss."

So out went the broadcast letters all over the world. They were not, however, to take the place of his personal letter-writing; he was still to toil late into the night, even though he continued to get up at four or four-thirty each morning. Keeping his desk cleared, and getting down to the bottom of the boxes piled under it—these were feats that gratified him intensely.

He always took a large number of monthly and weekly periodicals, as well as half a dozen newspapers. And the magazines, which he passed along to be read in the Home, gave him considerable trouble: the difficulty was the improper pictures they contained. He objected vigorously to illustrations that bore an "immodest suggestion, by reason of indecent dress or wanton expression." These he called "inviting and lewd" and unfit to meet the eyes of his people. Therefore all such must be clipped from the pages before the magazines entered the Home. He found indecency especially "in the advertising matter," and the need for reform "wide, great, and horrible." So we get another picture: of Brother Joseph at eighty bending over his desk until late every night, à la Anthony Comstock, hunting for bathing beauties and hosiery houris that might lead his lepers astray. He admitted, himself, that he was "cranky" on the subject, but attributed his intense feeling to his memory of the "evil ways" he had indulged in, fifty years earlier. He considered that "the soul is greatly injured by . . . too much seeing of the human form."

Even Edison was to be rebuked, it seems, though indecency is not usually associated with that eminent scientist. We have mentioned the phonograph that he sent to the Baldwin Home, with some twelve hundred records. A generous and fine gift, surely; but unhappily it brought in its wake a monthly catalog of new records—and this catalog regularly bore on its cover "naughty cuts, pretty bad (or pretty and bad) pictures. I cut them all out, and pasted them around a fine picture of Mr. Edison and sent it to him." One wonders whether Edison ever learned why Brother Joseph sent him this curious composition; but it bore fruit in a gift of fifty new records, with "a beautiful letter," and—

"we have lived in peace ever after. I don't see much change on the covers, at that, though now they are not really bad, only foolish and silly."

During these closing years he was writing articles occasionally, though not for pay. He confessed that he was "no writer at all," and would not accept money for what was printed. When a check for fifteen dollars was fairly forced on him by one editor, he wrote

that "it goes into my little fund for special help to
lepers. I have not accepted a cent of personal com-
pensation since coming here." For the Catholic Encyclopedia he did an article on Molokai, and several
scientific and historical articles for small magazines.
But write the story of his life he would not. That was
to be left for others to do, if they cared to, from the
notes that he left.

It was a continual pleasure to him to remember the
birthdays and wedding-days that were recorded in the
little brown address-book. His gifts were tiny and
unpretentious—strange shells, native canes, little
Madonna cameos, sometimes his own photographs—
but they were always accompanied by a few words of
friendly greeting. The wish that he always sent on a
wedding anniversary—"I hope for your happiness"—
must sometimes have roused a reminiscent pang. But
he often confessed ruefully that he feared he got more
pleasure out of sending these things than his friends
did from receiving them. "It is a sort of feeling that
I have had all my life, and will no doubt never out-
grow, to desire at once—on the receipt of anything that
gives me pleasure—to divide it with my friends, and
bring them in to share it. No doubt I have enhanced
the misery of a good many people by this trait, loading
on them things that gave no pleasure, or very little. It
can hardly be called generosity, but rather a lack of
consideration—I can often see it must be that way.
Something very pleasing—'Ah, So-and-So will enjoy
that'—and I hurry it off, or part of it."

Honors came to him in these autumn years, honors that thrilled him with a child-like gratification. The fleet paid him a visit, as already described. Then in 1926 a junior high school newly built by the Catholic parish of St. Jude in Beloit, not far from his old Wisconsin home, was named the Brother Dutton School. The rector of the parish and the school, the Rev. Joseph Hanz, wrote that they wished to honor him thus because he had spent his childhood near Beloit and had enlisted for the Civil War from their own county seat, Janesville. Brother Joseph replied that they could do it if they wanted to but that he did not deserve the honor. Then, when the cornerstone was laid, a number of veterans were present, among them three from Ira Dutton's old regiment, the 13th. He sent a flag to the school, which was raised at the dedication ceremony. The students coined a motto for themselves to symbolize Brother Joseph's life of service—*Fraira,* a combination of the Italian word for Brother and Dutton's original given name. As this chapter is being written in 1931, word comes that the new city high school in Beloit is to be called the Brother Dutton High School.

But "the most amazing and most gracious thing that ever happened" to him was to come through a still night of April in 1929. He was called to the telephone to take a call from the wireless office at Kalaupapa. The radio message was from his close friend, Rev. John Wynne of New York City:

"MESSAGE JUST RECEIVED FROM THE HOLY FATHER TO THE VENERABLE BROTHER DUTTON. THE HOLY FATHER CONFERS MOST CORDIALLY A SPECIAL APOSTOLIC BENEDICTION AS A PLEDGE OF THE DIVINE ASSISTANCE. HE HAS YOUR RADIO PORTRAIT ON HIS DESK."

Need it be said that Brother Joseph was startled? What it meant to him is seen in the letter he sent to Father Wynne in reply:

"After the first bewilderment over the receipt of the wireless message from Rome (last lap was by telephone), am again plodding on as usual. With a tender feeling toward the Holy Father, I am wishing to express, through you, deep gratitude for his great message, hoping to be always fully aware of its spiritual benefit to me. They said the Holy Father (God bless him!) has my little photo on his writing-desk."

And in a letter to a Protestant friend—

"The blessing from the Holy Father touched me deeply. I have been blessed for the little I have tried to do. Truly life has been good to me here."

The State, also, like the Church, was to pay him honor. In this same year the Hawaiian Legislature voted a resolution unanimously recording its appreciation "of the great and inspiring influence for good, the effective and splendid service rendered, during the past forty years by Brother Joseph Dutton in the Settlement of Molokai." We are told that, when a copy of this resolution reached him, he looked gravely at the paper and shook his head slowly. "They honor me too much," he said.

He was ill then, lying on the cot that was one of the only two bits of furniture in his room. A few days later he was visited by twenty members of the legislature and the Governor. Of this he wrote, when he sent the Semmes family in Memphis his copy of the resolution, "They paid me a visit—paid, or made—a jolly morning visit, headed by the Governor." That such homage should have evoked from him only so mild a comment as this cannot but raise certain questions in our minds. Why was he apparently not impressed, as another man would have been? Was it because he was growing old and tired, and slow in his reactions? Or was it due to his incurable self-depreciation, which led him to wonder constantly why so much should be made of the work he was doing?

Some day a cynical writer will take all the events of Brother Joseph's life and try to explain his motives and actions on some psychological basis. He will make much of Brother Joseph's censorship of magazines and papers, and of his lament over the so-called sins of his youth, and the "wild days." But one thing that writer will be unable to do, and that is to find any more material that will afford him a greater insight into Brother Joseph's life. The questions will be raised: why did he keep all the clippings about himself? why send pictures of his mother to strangers? That writer will even refuse to believe that the lay brother told the truth when, sending a printed ac-

THE DUTTON SCHOOL, BELOIT, WISCONSIN

count of his life to Rev. John G. Dutton, he said, "I have never read it." He will question whether the lay brother's modesty was so real as it appeared, ask why it was that he sent clippings about himself to hundreds of people. He may even say—it has already been said—that perhaps Brother Joseph's whole life at Molokai was but a bid for fame, an effort to capture the mantle that had fallen from Damien's shoulders.

But an honest interpretation of the documents in existence, by the light of common sense, shows Joseph Dutton to have been genuinely humble, devout, industrious, loyal, and easy to get along with; an ideal helper for Father Damien and equally an ideal administrator of the work after Damien's death. His cheerful simplicity was spontaneous, never forced. His humor was irrepressible. "I am an old, old relic," he wrote toward the end of his life, "still on duty, and happy. Almost ashamed to say how jolly I am. Often think, we don't know whether Our Lord ever laughed; but mine is ready to burst out any moment."

In his last illness, just before he was taken to Honolulu, he felt that he must summon strength enough to answer a friend who had written to him that the sacrifice had been too great. He wrote but a few words, but they are full of feeling:

"You speak of the glory of old age. Yes, but I am near the blessed peace of death. And I hold that I never made any real sacrifice in coming here. I have been blessed for it."

This view of a life of self-sacrifice typifies what it is so hard, often, for the Protestant mind to understand in the "religious," as Catholics call the men and women who enter monastic orders: a serene joy in a service that, to people still "in the world," looks like the dreariest of drudgery. Yet Brother Joseph, for all his passionate devotion to his Church, had never a streak of intolerance in him. "I am begging you," he once wrote to a number of young people, "to lead quiet, industrious, and sober lives. Be honest, always helping your neighbor for his own good. And be tolerant of the views of others concerning religion." May we not find here one reason why his associations with persons of all sorts at Molokai were amicable, if not indeed cordial? And why, in the letter quoted just above, he said that he had "never been lonesome here"?

# CHAPTER XIV

## BROTHER TO EVERYBODY

It seems almost absurd to discuss the testamentary dispositions of a man who owned no property, real or personal. But Brother Joseph decided to make a will; and what gives the decision interest is its preliminaries. He had refused the pension due him after the Civil War on the ground that "my country has always treated me far better than I deserve and does not owe me a cent. . . . Though urged many times to apply, have never consented to have any step taken. I have in a joking way said that, when they pass it around as an honorarium, I shall put it in the cabinet as a souvenir." Then suddenly, after all those years, he wrote to the Hon. George James of the Federal Reserve Board, asking that a pension be given him. But he was not expecting to use the money for himself—it was to go to charity, at the request of a stranger.

"I have often expressed hearty praise for the generous pension system of the Government, and have in fact helped some to get this needed assistance, while saying that so long as I could support myself [I] would never take one. Here I have the happy privilege of serving without pay, though the authorities are good enough to give me my bed and board. Uncle Sam compensated me well for the years of enlistment service and for a ten years' appointment after the Civil War, so [I] had never thought of applying for a pension.

"Now in 1911—twenty-five years after I came here—the citizens of a city in one of the States held a meeting to decide on means for keeping up a certain charity. A member suggested my pension, saying that I would not use it, so why not get it for this charity?—thinking, I presume, that anything Uncle Sam would pay should not be overlooked. So they wrote me about it. It hit me as a new idea. I sent the letter on to the Commissioner of Pensions at Washington. They made it a special case and rushed it through, and the pension checks came through, as I had consented at last.

"I had enlisted as Ira B. Dutton, and such was my name on the muster rolls. But they issued the pensions to Joseph Dutton, my new name. As the checks come, I endorse them, and they go back almost to where they were made. I never would have accepted for myself, thinking that one who could not behave right should not have a pension."

He does not mention either the city or the cause, and apparently felt no resentment in the matter. Not so Mrs. Semmes, his godmother, when she heard about it. For the city from which this remarkable proposal had emanated was her own, Memphis, and what the missionary's pension was wanted for was the community chest. Such are the methods of "drives"! Mrs. Semmes at once wrote her godson a long letter in protest; it made her very angry, she said, that anybody

should be so thoughtless (*thoughtless* is good) as to ask
him to give what could perfectly well have been given
by others, and ought to have been.  She reminded him
of the number of wealthy people of Memphis who
could afford to give nearly eight hundred dollars a
year far better than he, and whose connection with
local interests was considerably closer.  But Brother
Joseph did not see the affair as an imposition on his
kind heart.  "Since I would never use it," he told her,
"it might as well go to a good cause.  I never would
have thought of it if it had not been brought to my
attention."

The beneficiary of his pension checks was St. Cath-
erine's Industrial School in Memphis; to this the first
check went in 1911.  Early in 1912 the institution
passed into the hands of the Sisters of the Good Shepherd, and their convent received the money from 1912
until April, 1930.  At first the amount was small—in
1912 only $144.  But it was increased from time to
time until during the last years of his life it became
$65 a month.  Early in 1930 he could no longer sign
his name, and the checks were not returned to the
United States after that time.

But it was the endorsing of one of these pension
checks, at some date after the World War, that turned
his thoughts to the advisability of making a will.  At
the time he still had in the bank the last thousand dollars of his original funds, in the form of Liberty
Bonds.  And he may have wondered what would happen, after his death, to this money and to his collec-

tion of letters, curios, etc.  He therefore wrote to
W. O. Smith in Honolulu, telling him what he wanted
done with his effects after his death.  This letter of
three pages was, of course, not a real will, though it is
possible that the courts might later have construed it
as a holographic will, especially if the judge were one
who knew Brother Joseph and the circumstances.
However, the issue never arose because a proper will
was prepared later and duly signed by witnesses.  The
letter to Smith contains this statement:

"I am prompted to make this declaration concerning the matters with the Bank of Bishop, and certain
things after my passing away, in such manner that this
letter may serve as a will.  I have no real estate; my
interest in the family estate was conveyed to my
mother many years ago.  So this document relates
simply to my account in the Bishop Bank and to certain personal items, in case I do not get them disposed
of before death.  There are U. S. bonds of the Liberty
Loan, five, I think, of $200 each, and the total may be
applied to public welfare over the Islands, under your
advice.  My curios, a few hundred pounds, am intend-
ing to divide them between the following: State Historical Society, Madison; Cossitt Library Museum,
Memphis; Dartmouth College; and the Public Museum in Stowe, Vt., my birthplace."

The second will was made in 1927, and by this time
the thousand dollars in bonds had all been given to
charity.  But there were still left the items named in
a five-page typed list—his collection of letters and clip-

pings, which was very close to his heart. Shortly before his death he sent these to Father Wynne of New York, and much of this book is drawn from them. The list has interest in showing what kind of things Brother Joseph especially prized—photographs of his mother and of himself from boyhood onward; letters from his dearest friends and copies of his answers; his certificates of enlistment in the 13th Wisconsin, his Army commissions, medals, and badges; letters from W. O. Smith and from Mrs. Semmes; clippings from various papers relating to him and to the settlement. Altogether there are more than a thousand items, weighing over a hundred pounds; and nowhere among them is a reference to his marriage or divorce or to his feelings during the years of unhappiness.

It was while preparing this second will that he wrote: "Being dead a few times, periodically, in the newspapers, brought such a shower of rose-leaves in the form of nice letters that the whole becomes a sort of revelation. But when it's said so often, it's time to get ready."

And it is true that he was often to be reported dead, and as often that he was said to have contracted leprosy. Almost the first general news article about his going to the colony said briefly that he had the disease, and in an advanced stage. Mrs. Semmes at once wrote to him and was told promptly that the report was false; but his letter was written in a depressed mood and spoke unhopefully of the future—he anticipated that, like Damien, he would soon fall victim. But that mood seems to have passed, and the fear does not recur in any subsequent letter. It has been seen that he was extremely careful about infection.

When in 1913 the report went out that Brother Joseph had died, a flood of telegrams and letters poured in on the colony. "There was at least one happy thing about it," he commented; "one could read what people really thought about one." In 1921 a similar story was circulated, and he wrote, "I am still much alive, though getting used to the idea that I am not." A much more circumstantial article had appeared in December, 1919, which led him to protest that "modern newspapers must invent stories when there is no news." The *National Tribune* of Washington printed it first, and it was copied in many other papers. The headlines read: "Brother Dutton of Molokai, the Keeper of the Leper Colony, Retires from His Position," and the story following went into details about his having refused a pension, suddenly left the settlement, and gone to Honolulu for the rest of his days. The tone of his comment is as near indignation as he ever permitted himself: "I would not leave my lepers for all the money the world might have. I am happy here and never expect to leave."

Until 1920 he maintained the health record of which he had been so proud ever since he went through the Civil War without having reported on the sick-list. His physique and stamina were both remarkable. But in February, 1920, he was to share in the "flu" epidemic when it reached Molokai; "influenza

A REFLECTIVE MOOD ON THANKSGIVING DAY

of the old sort," he calls it, "with many trademarks of
the new. . . . Whatever it is, I just stay up and fight
it, though I have been really ill for the first time in
my life." Slight though it seemed to him, it left its
marks, and thenceforth he was to find the infirmities
of old age weighing more and more heavily. For years
he had been deaf in one ear and his sight had been
failing. Now a cataract began to form in one eye. It
was a time in which he could quite properly have
spared himself, for the colony was adequately manned
and he was seventy-seven years old. But he persisted
in his all-day working habits, and did not even forgo
his practice of writing letters until late at night. And
in spite of growing infirmity he developed an increased interest in the affairs of the world outside.

Magazines were piled high in his little study, mostly
American, some English. Most of these he paid for
himself, and two years in advance, after his provident
fashion. Newspapers have been mentioned. His
books were mostly works on geology, botany, and
medicine. The Catholic Encyclopedia, to which he
had contributed an article, was flanked by the Britan-
nica—these were given away by his will. A large part
of the printed matter that surrounded him consisted
of the reports and publications of the many organizations to which he belonged; for during the last years
of his life he had become a "joiner." The societies of
which he was a member constitute an imposing if
rather odd list.

As a member of the Society of Sanitary and Moral

Prophylaxis he wrote many letters to Dr. Morrow of New York.  He was a contributor to the McKinley Memorial.  He belonged to the Hawaiian Vigilance Corps, to the English-Speaking Union, to the American Rights League, to the American Red Cross.  But what interested him most was the State Historical Society of Wisconsin and the Grand Army of the Republic.  Not only did he send his dues and get all their publications, but to these two associations he sent various documents and curios for their museums.  The yearly reports of these two show signs of having been carefully read; many pages are marked.  Why he joined the International Longfellow Society we may not know, or the New York Committee for Constitutional Campaigns and Celebrations.  More easily understood is his membership in the International Council for Patriotic Service.

It is evident that during these last ten years he was reaching out toward the larger world, the world he had turned his back on forty years before.  And he was particularly interested in what he learned of the ideas held outside about the leper colony.  These came to him in various ways, but it took Jack London's visit to provoke him to commit to paper his feelings on the subject.  London made several visits to the settlement and in recording his experiences had laid on the colors pretty thick.  He met Brother Joseph—as we know from the writings themselves—but he was much less thrilled by the old man's character and career than in the horse-races, the fact that he had climbed over the cliff trail (as the postman did every time he brought the mail), and his glorious freedom from any fear of contracting leprosy. The statements he made subsequently about the settlement roused the protest of the colony officials, and Brother Joseph wrote in a letter: "The less said about London's visit, the better. After all, these people see the colony only for a few hours or days and know little about it."

Afterward he was writing as follows to another friend:

"There is much public misapprehension regarding Molokai. It is no longer a pest-hole, no longer a place of suffering. I think that those here are better—happier—than most natives on the Islands. They have good food, fine medical attention, amusements, the finest climate in the world, and the best attention from the authorities. Writers picture horrors, mostly in their own minds. Perhaps the world likes to hear of horrors more than of cheer. But it's not what it was in Damien's day, or when I first came. Up to 1902 or 1903 things [were] not good here; after that a great change, until today the place [is] as orderly, as happy, as any spot in the world. People write asking how they can help; many offer to come and work. I reply that neither money nor workers are needed. . . . They have movies, radios, even a few automobiles. I have not seen a flying-machine, but we have everything else."

The most dramatic event of these closing years was the flood in 1927.

"*Easter, 1927.*—Was there ever such a one before? Hardly. The first real flood in forty years came. The heavy downpour started about 5 A.M., following a rain that began the evening before. The great mountain-tops, ravines, and river-beds were filled. Except at this point all the flow passed into the ocean. Like an immense cloudburst the noble waters came pouring over the cliffs. It was grand! I crept like a little mouse down the steps of my cottage—the oldest building here—like myself, the oldest person. I crept between solid walls that stood while other walls were crumbling, heavy rocks rolling through our grounds, my eyes almost blinded by rain, when I saw approaching—what? who? Father Peter. He climbed a wall, wading, jumping over obstacles, still holding what he bore. What was it? It was My Lord, from the altar of the church.

" 'Getting to church too risky,' he said. 'Prepare here for Holy Communion.'

"I opened the office door, and in the rain and wind received my Lord. There came a calm, though water was still falling from the cliffs and rocks tumbling like giants. Bells began to ring, and Brother Jules, young and strong, hurried to a bench and I climbed up and he bore me to the church.

"Incidental items many: houses destroyed, cows driven to the beach to save them from being washed in sea, water system damaged, and weeks of repairing walls and buildings. Now the flood is a memory—and I have only a flood of letters to answer!"

The next year he was eighty-five, and the break-

down that came on him descended as suddenly as a
bolt of lightning.  His eyesight had failed, so that he
could no longer read; he often said that his memory,
too, was leaving him.  But he still kept busy.  One of
the tasks he would not delegate to others was the care
of the flag; each morning he ran it up, each evening he
took it down—and now it was noticed that when it
came fluttering down the pole he would catch it before
it could touch the ground, and for a moment hold it
pressed tightly against his body.  One August evening
—this is in 1928—he left his house at dusk to get the
flag.  Feeling, as he wrote, "a bit tired, and suddenly
cold, I dropped at the foot of the cottage steps to rest.
An active leper boy saw me there and ran for a
Brother.  What a joy to live among people who will
assist you in every need!  In a few moments Brother
Jules came, and quickly had me in bed, and relief
measures were at once begun.  For several days I lay
hovering over the great deep, life's hold very slender.
Praying to Almighty God and Saint Joseph night and
day was the sum of my effort.  Having always had a
hearty respect for the Angel of Death, a close acquaint-
ance caused personal affection."

It was pneumonia, and the beginning of the end.
True, he was to recover, to live for eighteen months
longer.  But at the moment it seemed doubtful
whether he would ever again leave his bed.  He rallied; but "it made no difference; after all, I was old
and my work was done.  But my friends, the doctors,
and Saint Joseph aided me."

Saint Joseph . . . What a warmth of feeling he always had in his heart for that saint! It was Saint Joseph's name that he had taken for his own long ago, and in the forty years since then he had developed a sort of tender intimacy with his patron that led him, in his letters, to speak of Saint Joseph as though he were a human friend who walked beside him and knew all his affairs. And now he promised the saint that if he were allowed to recover he would catch up with all his neglected correspondence. This duty became, therefore, his first care after he was out of bed.

But he could not, of course, attend to it himself. Friends suggested that he dictate a four-page letter, which they would have printed in Honolulu to send out to everybody to whom he owed an answer. And this last general letter went to more than four hundred persons in many parts of the world. With the friar who was caring for him, Brother Ludger, he discussed the preparation of this book from the material he was sending to Father Wynne in New York; and he sent messages to Frank Waterbury in Des Moines about the documents that would be forwarded later.

"We watched him night and day [Father Ludger records] for a long time. After that morning in August, 1928, he did not leave his house until his trip to Kalaupapa last spring, having been bedridden for two years. We took him to the territorial hospital at Kalaupapa, and they partly took a cataract away from Brother Joseph's eye. He remained there for about one week. It was a hard trial for the old man; he did

HOISTING THE FLAG

not feel at home in the hospital. It was his first trip in many years—thirty-five or more. He had never left Kalawao, and for the first time was in an automobile. Then after a week we took him back. Many nights we had long talks—about the book, about him, about his life. But he was very sick."

Brother Ludger speaks of his having been bedridden; this is not quite accurate, for he could and did leave his bed at times. Colonel R. M. Blanchard, one of the few who saw Brother Joseph during this last illness, says that when he entered the house he found him lying on "a pallet in a crude shed; and though weak and sick he insisted on rising, and led me to his little workroom littered with correspondence." And Brother Joseph himself wrote, after this illness, "Though not out, I spend some time at my desk."

Brother Ludger goes on:

"We brought him back to his house, and then he complained of a trouble and could not sleep. We had an X-ray made and found he suffered from gravel. The doctors decided to take him to the hospital at Honolulu, but we had an awful hard time to get his consent. First he refused absolutely, but I made him understand the necessity of the trip. Forty-four years had gone by since he saw Honolulu last. So on July 4 Brother Joseph and I took the steamer. In the morning, at half-past ten, we left Kalaupapa, and arrived in Honolulu the next day."

Long ago Brother Joseph had expressed the wish that he might die at the colony, and he was now ob-

durate against argument until the officials of the Board
of Health came and added their weight; then he gave
in.   How he should be taken to the main island, in his
condition, was a problem; it seems that an airplane
was considered.   But in the end, as Brother Ludger
records, he went by the steamer.   And his old, blind
eyes could not see the cliffs that he was leaving behind.

At the Honolulu dock there were—of course!—
reporters.   Reporters by the dozen, pelting the
dying man with inane questions: what did he think
about the changes in the world; was there any hope
that leprosy could be cured?   Most of these questions
he ignored, though to one he replied by saying, "I
think Our Lord cured the last leper"; and presently
the reporters left him in peace.   Forty-four years ago
he had set out from this same dock, a stalwart man in
the prime of life.   Now he was lifted by a sailor—the
worn, frail body was no great weight—and carried to
the waiting automobile.   He smiled at the people who
were gathered to see him.   Then St. Francis's Hospital, his room fragrant with flowers, many of them from
persons he had never heard of.

"Everything," he commented to his companion,
"everything goes like a wiz nowadays.   It's a fine day,
and I feel the sun.   I regret nothing—but I forget
many things.   Regret nothing but the evil in the
world, and leprosy.   A cure for that?   I doubt it very
much.   I'm blind and deaf, and I guess I'm almost
senseless.   But I have no regrets."

The trip left him weakened further, and for several

days he was allowed to see few visitors. Only the
Governor and some other high officials were admitted
to the room. A friend who saw him on August 15
wrote:

"I found his mind a complete blank. He cannot
seem to grasp anything. He has several complaints,
cannot get better, and is much too feeble to operate
on. They try to make him just as happy as they can
until the end. This will not be long."

The visitor was mistaken: Brother Joseph was to
gain strength after a few weeks, though it was a hard
pull. It was during these weeks that he began to wonder whether God would forgive his "wasted life," to
dwell again on the "wrongdoing" of his earlier life.
He seems now to have had but two thoughts in a mind
that could no longer recognize his friends: Would
God accept the years of service as penance? And
could he—*when* could he—return to his leper boys?

By the first of October he was better and his memory was stronger. To callers he spoke often of his
early life, of his war days and his work for the Government. His manner was sane and calm, his thin body
erect, his white skin and beard and hospital robe giving him the aspect of a saint. Letters poured in, and
the Sister was kept busy reading them aloud. They
must be put on the bureau—he was going to answer
them all. Suddenly he announced that it was time for
a second operation on his eyes. They told him he was
too weak—it might not be successful. No matter: they

were *his* eyes, and he was going to find out whether anything could be done about them. And have the operation he did—successfully.

How far his sight was restored by it is a question. He was driven to a doctor's office—being now able to leave the hospital temporarily—and he was fitted with new glasses, powerful glasses that enabled him to see objects in his room and to distinguish his friends. But a letter that went to Des Moines in December said that he could not see clearly, and could not read at all. At least, however, he was no longer totally blind, and this cheering assurance brought measurable improvement in his general condition. Even his hearing was remarkably improved. All these things were encouraging, but they did not touch the main difficulty. The public had been told that his purpose in coming to Honolulu was to save his eyesight; the truth was that he was suffering from an incurable organic trouble, though he wanted nothing said about it.

Then, astonishingly, he declared that he wanted a radio in his room. Heretofore radios had meant nothing to him because he could not hear. But now—well, need it be said that the public, hearing his wish, instantly provided a radio powerful enough to get stations on both sides of the Pacific? Another surprise for his friends was the keen interest he developed in football. Since he had never seen a game, we can but wonder how he pictured it in his mind. His radio brought him the running accounts of the games, and for a while he was able to listen.

Then one day, his mind grew weak again; he fancied he had been called to Rome, that he was spending his time there examining old documents and reading the records of the past. Such periods alternated with intervals of clarity during which he would turn again to his radio for entertainment.

His last Christmas brought a shower of letters, cards and gifts from all over the world, and he got a faint but evident pleasure from having them read and described to him. He was not unhappy; the Sisters say that he did not once complain, and spent much of his time in prayer. His pathetically hopeful plan for returning to Molokai involved the use of an airplane. "It will be my first and my last ride," he said. When he could not sleep at night he would ask the Sister to read some letter that had come that day, and then to put it away carefully "so that I can answer it." To his good friend in Des Moines he sent a message: "God bless you—for you and I will have a long talk in a few months, by May at least."

The new year came, the eighty-eighth of Brother Joseph's life. His mind was clear and not troubled. We cannot use the word "resigned," because he had always been resigned to whatever God sent. Those near him often heard a little chuckle from his chair—none of them knew what thought was amusing the old man. In February the Hawaiian Government voted him a pension of $300 a month. Once, some years before, they had introduced a bill to a similar end, and had been told that he would not take the pension.

Nor did he need this one; his hospital expenses were being paid by the Board of Health, and he had no other wants. It was a happy gesture of sympathy from the Island people, but they were to be able to send him only one payment. Before he lapsed into coma the last sacraments were administered, and on March 26, 1931, after twenty-four hours of unconsciousness, he died. He was within a few days of his eighty-eighth birthday.

The funeral that was arranged was undoubtedly impressive, but we who know by now what kind of man Joseph Dutton was may be permitted to believe that a far simpler ceremony would have been his choice. Probably a spectacular funeral was inevitable, considering his position in the Islands and the vast numbers of people who mourned him. A flag was draped over his coffin—the flag he had loved for so many years—and other features, too, gave it the aspect of a military funeral. It was held in the Cathedral, which though large could not hold all who came that day to hear the solemn requiem mass sung over Brother Joseph's body, to honor the man whose long years of sacrifice had done so much to alleviate one of humanity's ancient evils. Among them were the highest political and military officials of the Islands. After the mass the coffin, attended by the 64th Artillery as escort, was taken to the cemetery and placed in a vault. (It was to be moved later to Kalawao, so that Brother Joseph might lie in the grounds of the Home he loved.)

Three times came the sharp reports from the firing-squad—then silence for a moment—then the bugle, sending forth the sad notes of Taps, the good-night call that Ira Dutton had listened to so many nights back in the '60's. Then it had sounded to the skies of his native land; now it filled the clear morning air of a tropic island in the Pacific. Its notes rose and fell; the last one died away; and the soldier who had fought the good fight was left to his last long rest.

And when his friends came to settle his estate according to the will he had left, they found no estate to settle: what he had had a few years ago had by now been given away, all of it. The executor's hands were empty.

But did Brother Joseph leave nothing? Money had counted for little to him during his life, it should be counted as nothing at his death. The estate that he did leave cannot be reckoned in dollars and cents, cannot be handled. It consists in a memory and an example. A memory of self-abnegating sacrifice, an example of heroism in the face of difficulties, which earn him a place beside Father Damien in history. The story of Molokai is the story of these two men. No such opportunity as they had will ever come again, probably, for leprosy may soon be on its way to the limbo of diseases that man has forever banished. The Molokai colony may come to be regarded as we of the 20th century regard the lazar houses of the 12th—as merely an interesting bit of bygone history. But the names of Damien and of Dutton cannot but live.

If the author of this book has any faith at all, it is

one that is very far away from the faith that brought peace and comfort to these two men.    But somehow he feels confident that the Church they served, whose memory is so long, whose appreciation of noble service is so kindly, will give them the honor that is their due: forgiving and forgetting Damien's waywardness, his temper, the restless impatience that made him a man, and remembering only the service and the heroism that made him a saint; and that in canonizing Damien it will set by his side among the Saints of the Church his friend and helper, Brother Joseph.    Damien is known the world over as the Apostle to the Lepers. Let us remember Joseph Dutton by the name that he called himself—Brother to Everybody.

# BIBLIOGRAPHY

# BIBLIOGRAPHY

A COMPLETE list of the sources consulted by the author in writing this book, manuscript and printed, would require almost a volume to itself.

*Original Sources*—Two-thirds of the book is based on private documents that cannot be listed in a bibliography. The principal collection has been the letters and manuscripts brought together by Brother Joseph during his forty-four years at the leper colony—a library of original material dealing not only with his own life but also with Father Damien's last years and death. The second manuscript source was the large private collection of letters from Brother Joseph to the late Frank Waterbury, of Des Moines, Iowa.

*Printed Sources*—I shall give only a summary list of printed sources—practical rather than exhaustive; allowing the student to trace the statements in the book to their origins, and the general reader to explore further any bypaths that interest him. It will be noticed that newspaper and magazine articles about Brother Joseph have not been included; they are largely untrustworthy. As for the sources of the passages on medieval leprosy and the leper mass, and more particularly the medical treatment of leprosy (which is touched upon only briefly), the books listed are the most important and most readily accessible. Many other works have been consulted—articles in medical periodicals, bulletins, and Government documents—but these have been omitted. To readers desiring a more exhaustive bibliography on leprosy we suggest the excellent "Index-Catalogue of the Surgeon General's Office," Washington, D. C., in its several editions.

HELEN HARPER ATEN.

ALLEN, JAMES LANE, *Flute and Violin and Other Kentucky Tales and Romances*. New York, 1905.

*Annual Report of the Adjutant General of the State of Wisconsin for the Year Ending December 30th, 1865*. Madison, Wis., 1866.

BALLANTYNE, ARCHIBALD, *Father Damien and the Lepers*, in *The Living Age*, vol. 181. May 25, 1889.

BLANCHARD, R. M., *A Day at Kalaupapa*, in *The Military Surgeon*, vol. 65. Sept., 1929.

BOND, FRANCIS, *Introduction to English Church Architecture from the Eleventh to the Sixteenth Century*. 2 vols. London, 1913.

BROWN, WILLIAM FISKE, *Rock County, Wisconsin: a New History of Its Cities, Villages, Towns, Citizens and Varied Interests, From the Earliest Times Up to Date*. 2 vols. Chicago, 1908.

CAMERON, CHARLOTTE, *Two Years in Southern Seas*. Boston, n.d.

CARMICHAEL, D. A., *Report on Leprosy in the Hawaiian Islands*, in *Public Health Reports* (issued by the Supervising Surgeon General, Marine Hospital Service, Washington, D. C.), vol. 13, no. 52. 1898.

CLIFFORD, EDWARD, *Father Damien*. London, 1889.

COULTON, GEORGE GORDON (compiled by): *Social Life in Britain from the Conquest to the Reformation*.

Cambridge, 1918.

CRAVEN, MME. AUGUSTUS (*née* La Ferronnays), *Le Père Damien.* Paris, 1900.

CUTTS, EDWARD LEWES, *Parish Priests and Their People in the Middle Ages in England.* London, 1898.

—— *Scenes and Characters of the Middle Ages.* London, 1886.

DAVIS, C. E., *Leprosy in the Hawaiian Islands,* in *Albany Medical Annals,* vol. 22. Feb., 1901.

DITCHFIELD, PETER HAMPSON, *The Story of Our English Towns.* London, 1907.

DONAHUE, GEORGE J., *Damien and Reform.* Boston, 1921.

DULISCOUET, EUGÈNE-HYACINTHE, *Les Lépreux au Moyen Âge en France.* Bordeaux, 1906.

ELLIS, HENRY HAVELOCK, *Studies in the Psychology of Sex.* 7 vols. Philadelphia, 1901-1928.

FAY, HENRY-MARCEL, *Histoire de la Lèpre en France; Lépreux et Cagots du Sud-Ouest.* Paris, 1910.

FITCH, JOHN, *Annals of the Army of the Cumberland.* Philadelphia, 1864.

GASQUET, FRANCIS AIDEN, *Parish Life in Medieval England.* London, 1906.

GATEWOOD, J. D., *A Visit to the Leper Settlement, Molokai, Hawaii,* in *United States Naval Medical Bulletin,* vol. 5. Jan., 1911.

GEROULD, KATHARINE FULLERTON, *Hawaii, Scenes and Impressions.* New York, 1916.

GOODHUE, E. S., *The Molokai Leper Settlement,* in *The Medical Record,* vol. 92, Oct. 13, 1917.

GUERNSEY, ORRIN, and WILLARD, J. F., *History of Rock County, and Transactions of the Rock County Agricultural Society and Mechanics' Institute.* Janesville, Wis., 1856.

HANNAH, IAN CAMPBELL, *Christian Monasticism: a Great*

*Force in History.* New York, 1925.

*Hawaii. Board of Health. Report of the President of the Board of Health to the Legislative Assembly of 1886.* Honolulu, H. I., 1886.

HULME, EDWARD MASLIN, *The Middle Ages.* New York, 1929.

HYDE, HENRY KNIGHT, *Charles McEwen Hyde: a Memorial Prepared by His Son.* Ware, Mass., 1901.

JOHNSTONE, ARTHUR, *Recollections of Robert Louis Stevenson in the Pacific.* London, 1905.

LIVEING, ROBERT, *Elephantiasis Græcorum, or True Leprosy.* London, 1873.

LONDON, CHARMIAN KITTREDGE, *Our Hawaii.* New York, 1917.

LONDON, JACK, *The Lepers of Molokai,* in *The Contemporary Review,* vol. 95, March, 1909.

LOVEJOY, DANIEL B., *From Youth to Age; Adventures in a Varied Life; History of the 13th Wisconsin Infantry Regiment.* Chicago, 1894.

LYON, ADELIA C., *Reminiscences of the Civil War, Compiled From the War Correspondence of Colonel William P. Lyon.* San Jose, Cal., 1907.

McCOY, G. W., *A Brief History of Leprosy in Hawaii,* in *The Military Surgeon,* vol. 33, Dec., 1913.

MARTÉNE (EDMOND MARTENIUS), *De Antiquis Ecclesiæ Ritibus.* III, x. Venetiis, 1783.

MERCIER, CHARLES ARTHUR, *Leper Houses and Medieval Hospitals: Being the Fitzpatrick Lectures, Delivered Before the Royal College of Physicians, London, 5 and 10 November, 1914.* London, 1915.

MOURITZ, ARTHUR ALBERT ST. M., *The Path of the Destroyer; a History of Leprosy in the Hawaiian Islands.* Honolulu, H. I., 1916.

MUIR, ERNEST, *Handbook on Leprosy.* Cuttack, India, 1921.

MUNRO, DANA CARLETON, *The Middle Ages, 395-1272.* New York, 1921.

NEWMAN, GEORGE, and EHLERS, EDWARD, and IMPEY, S. P., *Prize Essays on Leprosy.* London, 1895.

O'DAY, J. C., *A Visit to the Leper Colony of Molokai, Hawaii,* in *The Urologic and Cutaneous Review,* vol. 19, May, 1915.

PAMPHILE, FATHER (edited by), *Life and Letters of Father Damien, the Apostle to the Lepers.* London, 1889.

QUILLER-COUCH, SIR ARTHUR THOMAS, *Victors of Peace: Florence Nightingale—Pasteur—Father Damien.* New York, 1927.

QUINLAN, MAY, *Damien of Molokai.* London, 1909.

ROGERS, SIR LEONARD, and MUIR, ERNEST, *Leprosy.* London, 1925.

SENN, NICHOLAS, *Father Damien, the Leper Hero.* Chicago, 1905.

SHAW, HENRY, *Dresses and Decorations of the Middle Ages.* 2 vols. London, 1843.

SIMPSON, SIR JAMES YOUNG, *Antiquarian Notices of Leprosy and Leper Hospitals in Scotland and England,* in *The Edinburgh Medical and Surgical Journal,* vols. 56 and 57, 1841 and 1842.

STEUART, JOHN ALEXANDER, *Robert Louis Stevenson: a Critical Biography.* 2 vols. Boston, 1924.

STEVENSON, ROBERT LOUIS, *Prince Otto—Island Nights' Entertainments—Father Damien.* Vol. 4 of *The Novels and Tales of Robert Louis Stevenson.* New York, 1909.

STODDARD, CHARLES WARREN, *Apostrophe to the Skylark—The Bells of San Gabriel—Joe of Lahaina—Father Damien Among the Lepers.* Los Angeles, 1909.

—— *The Lepers of Molokai.* Notre Dame, Ind., 1885.

TEELING, BARTLE, *Father Damien,* in *The American Catholic Quarterly Review,* vol. 15, Oct., 1890.

THOMPSON, J. A. and CANTLIE, JAMES, *Prize Essays on Leprosy.* London, 1897.

THORNDIKE, LYNN, *A History of Magic and Experimental Science During the First Thirteen Centuries of Our Era.* 2 vols. New York, 1923.

*United States Treasury Department. Public Health Reports, vol. 45, no. 13. Clinical Records of 65 Cases of Recovery from Leprosy.* Washington, D. C., 1930.

VAN HORNE, THOMAS B., *History of the Army of the Cumberland.* 2 vols. Cincinnati, 1875.

WALSH, J. J., *Leper Hospitals of the Middle Ages; the Eradication of a Great Endemic Disease,* in *Hospital Progress,* vol. 4, 1923.

WISHART, ALFRED WESLEY, *A Short History of Monks and Monasteries.* Trenton, N. J., 1900.